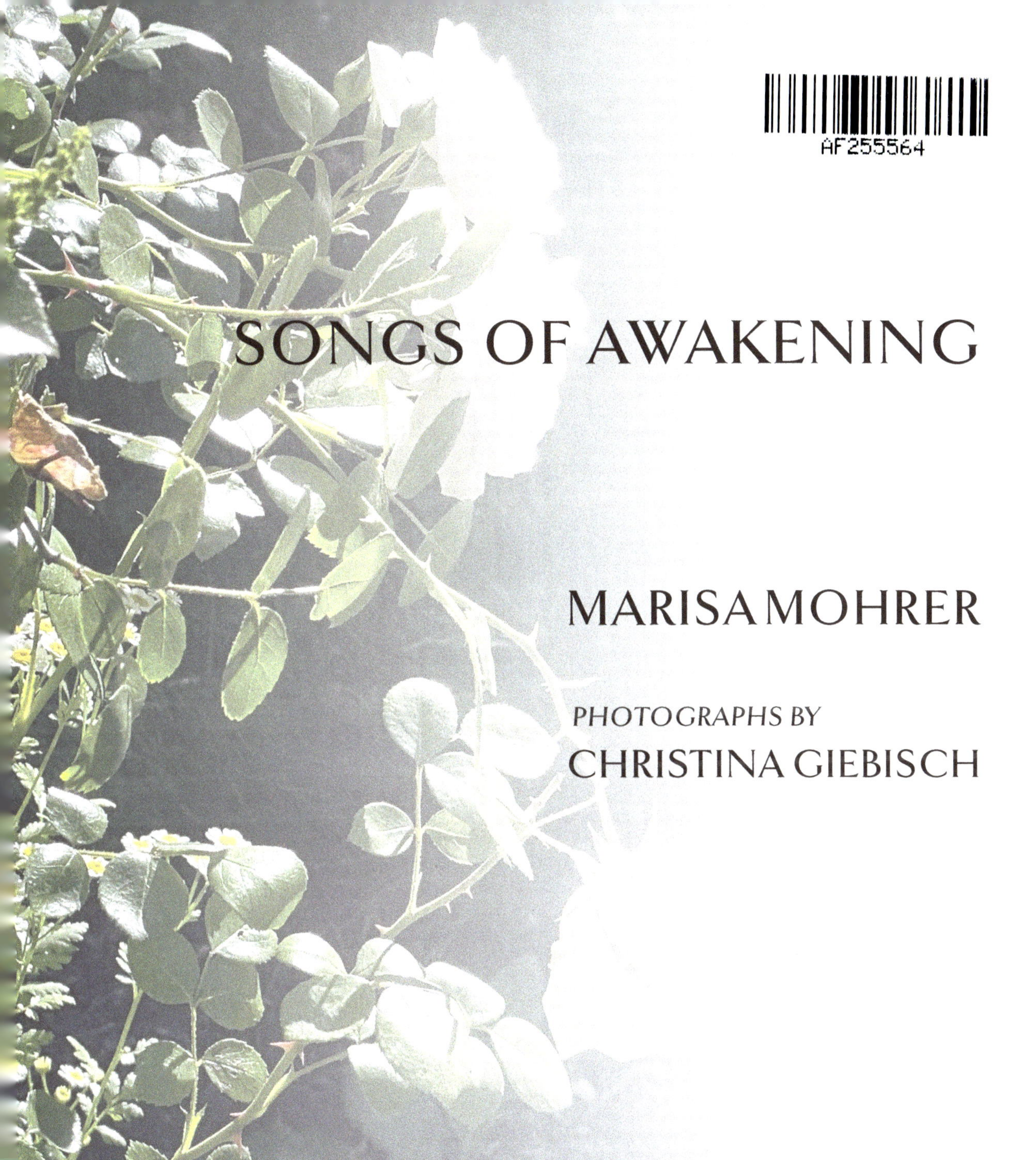
SONGS OF AWAKENING
MARISA MOHRER
PHOTOGRAPHS BY
CHRISTINA GIEBISCH
AF255564

"Marisa Mohrer stunningly transmits aspects of the Mystery with each poem, speaking from what she knows in the depth of her Being. These pointers move the heart deeply, encouraging transcendence of the everyday mind and evoking contact with our deeper nature. Her 'songs of awakening' carry on an ancient tradition, helping modern seekers touch the freedom of realization."

TINA RASMUSSEN, PhD, co-author of *Practicing the Jhanas*

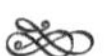

"Each poem in this collection is a portal into the mystery . . . a meditation on encountering this living, dying world with freshness, courage, and wonder."

TARA BRACH, PhD, author of *Radical Acceptance*
and *Radical Compassion*

"*Songs of Awakening* fulfills the promise of the title. This wonderful collection of poems points to the experience of awakening with such grace and simplicity that it opens the way to our own deepening realization."

JOSEPH GOLDSTEIN, author of *Mindfulness:
A Practical Guide to Awakening*

"These profound poems are like windows into the ultimate. They come from and draw us into a depth of awakening. They can be read again and again, each time a fresh opening."

RICK HANSON, PhD, *New York Times* bestselling author of *Hardwiring Happiness* and *Buddha's Brain*

"In *Songs of Awakening*, Marisa Mohrer shares her heart through this collection of lovely poems. Poems to be read, re-read, and savored, a pleasure to read and contemplate as we move deeper into listening to our hearts and minds."

SHARON SALZBERG, *New York Times* bestselling author of *Real Happiness*

"Marisa Mohrer reveals her first awakening to us through her beautiful words. Each poem points the reader toward that mystery tucked deeply in our consciousness—the source of all, the Absolute. Journey with Mohrer as she touches into and reveals her direct experience of awakening."

STEPHEN MUGEN SNYDER, Roshi, Zen and Theravada lineage teacher; author of *Demystifying Awakening*, *Buddha's Heart*, *Trust in Awakening*, and *Liberating the Self*; co-author of *Practicing the Jhanas*

to my teacher, Tina Rasmussen, for pointing the way

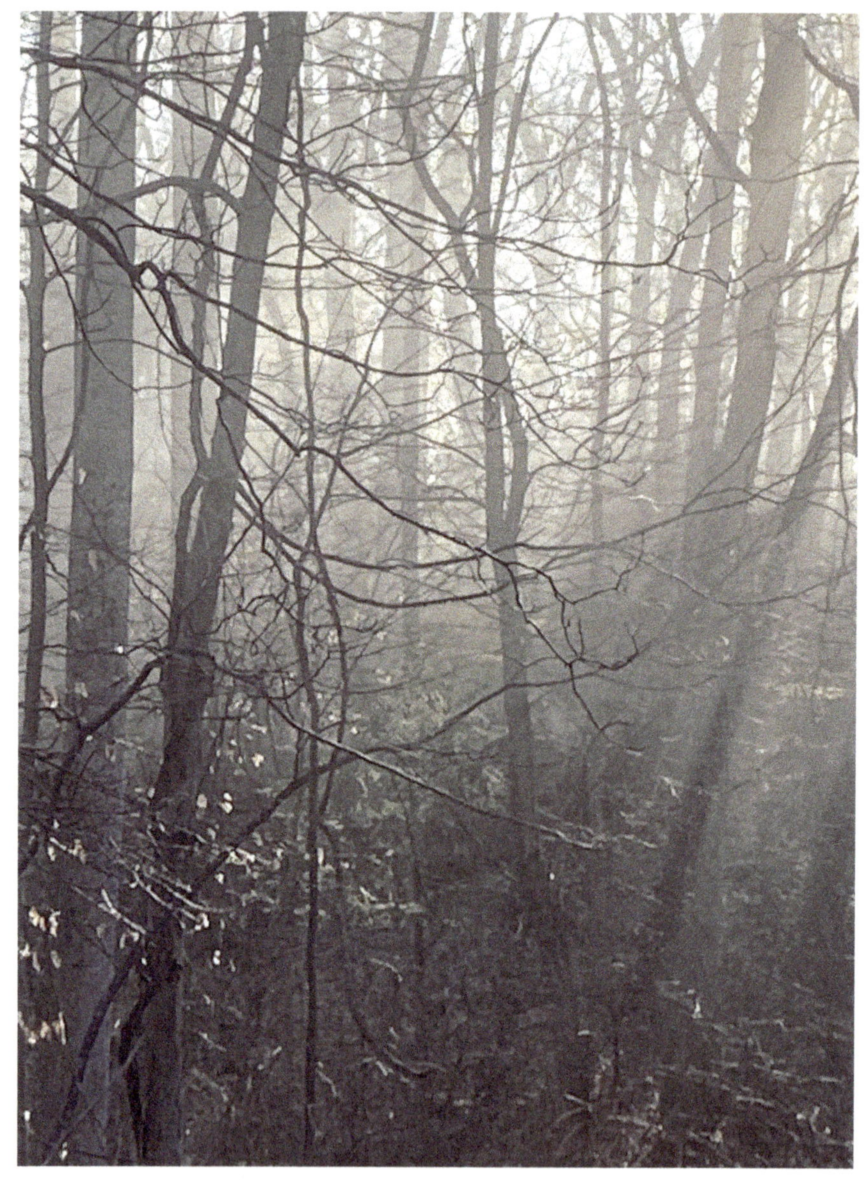

Preface

Every moment matters.

Songs of Awakening evolved over a six-year period in the process of uncovering the unified integration of mind with reality. The teachings captured in this book unexpectedly arose while Marisa was training in meditation practices during long periods of silent retreat. In the pages ahead, you will find carefully matched photographs taken by her mother, Christina Giebisch. It is their hope that the braiding together of images and text offers you a new landscape through which to explore the expansive terrain of the human experience. Each poem stands as an invitation to open the door to a sense of embodied spaciousness, wonder, and possibility.

Step in.

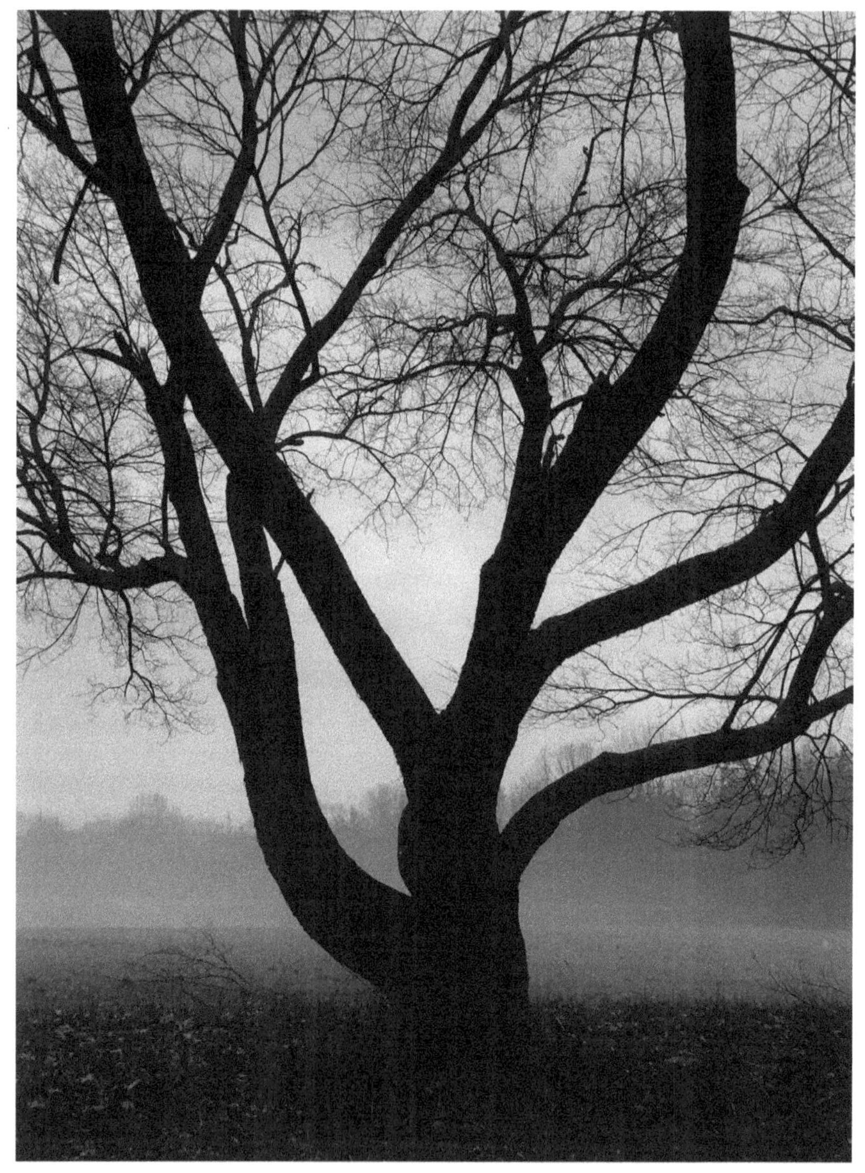

One Unified Body.
One Unified Being.

This is the nature of our reality.

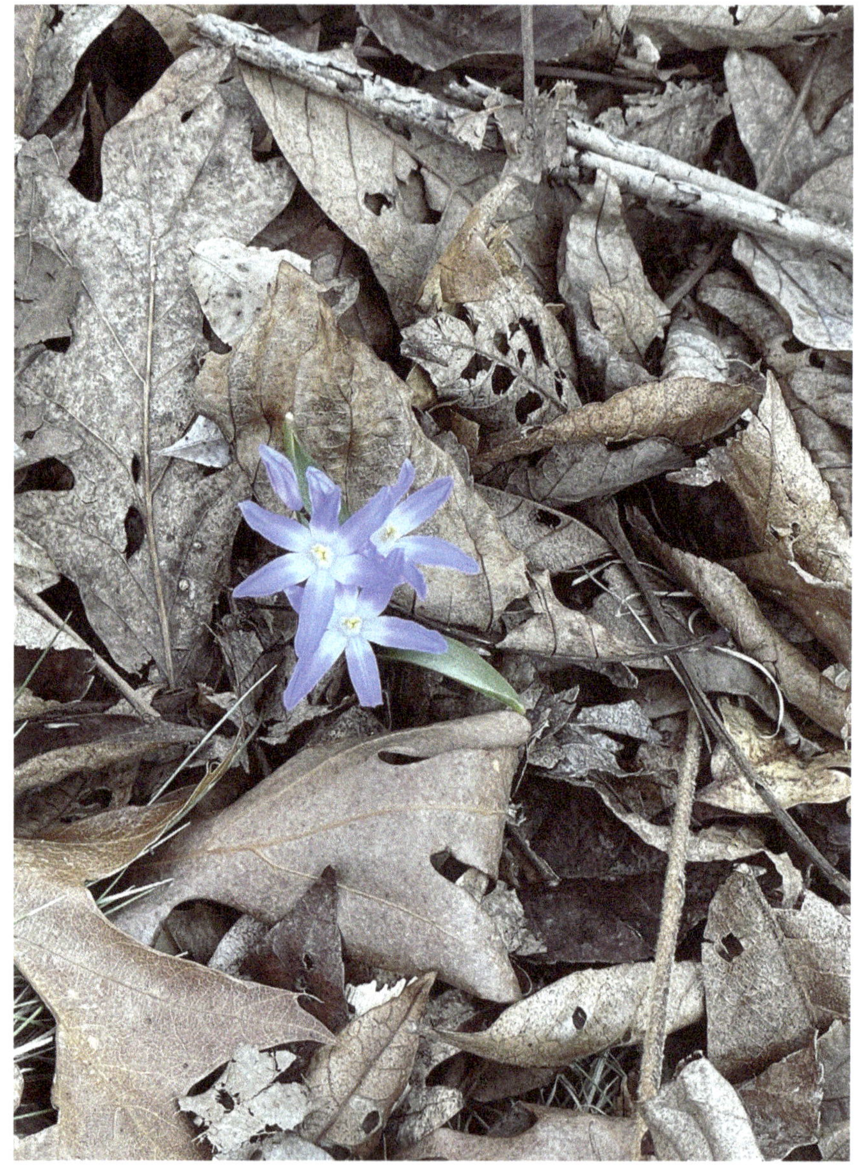

The deepest intelligence we possess
lies beyond
the thinking mind.

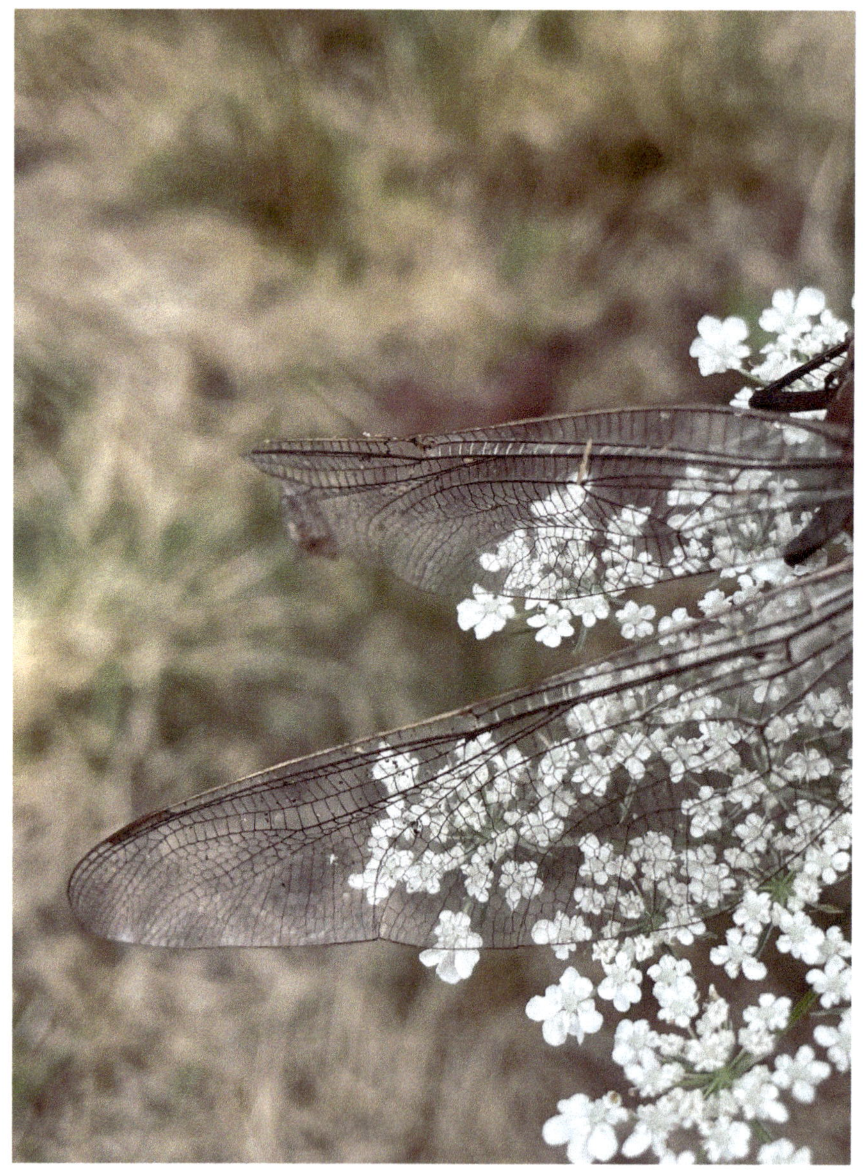

Meditation can heal our most pervasive suffering:
the illusory perception of separation
from everything and everyone around us.

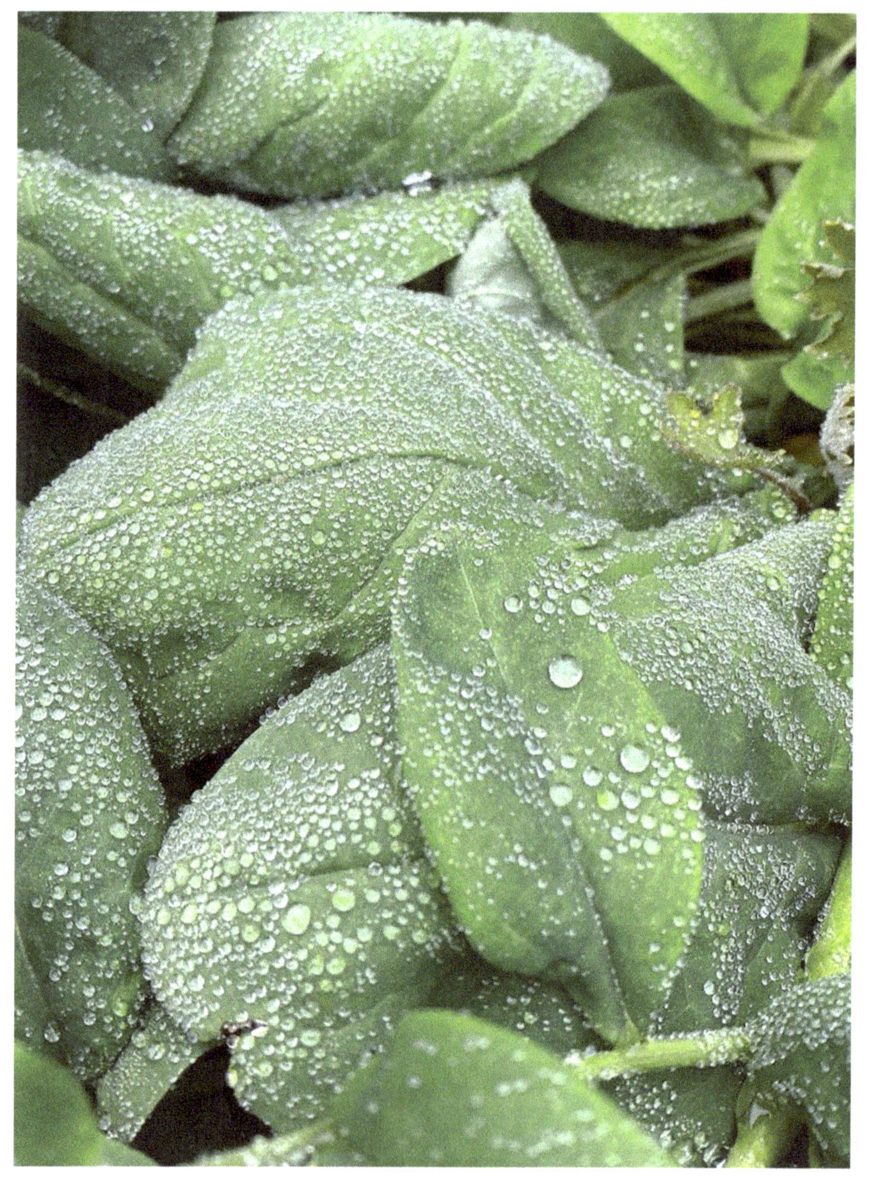

Everything and everyone

lives within you.

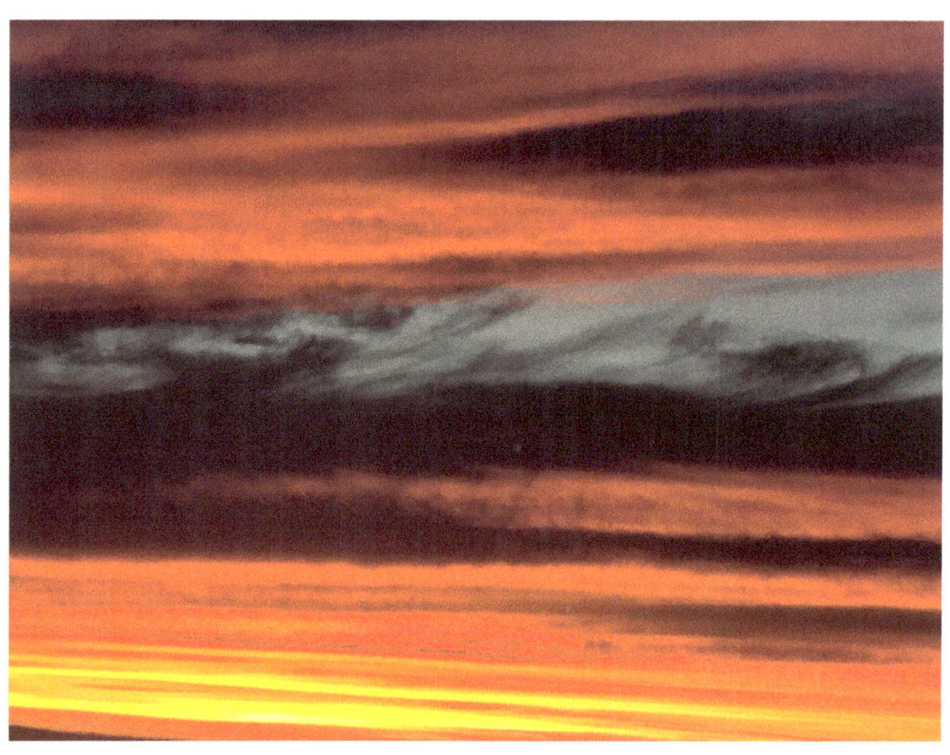

Drive off into the distance.
Send the maps flying out the window
and into the wind.

Freedom is not at the end of the endless road.

It is here now.

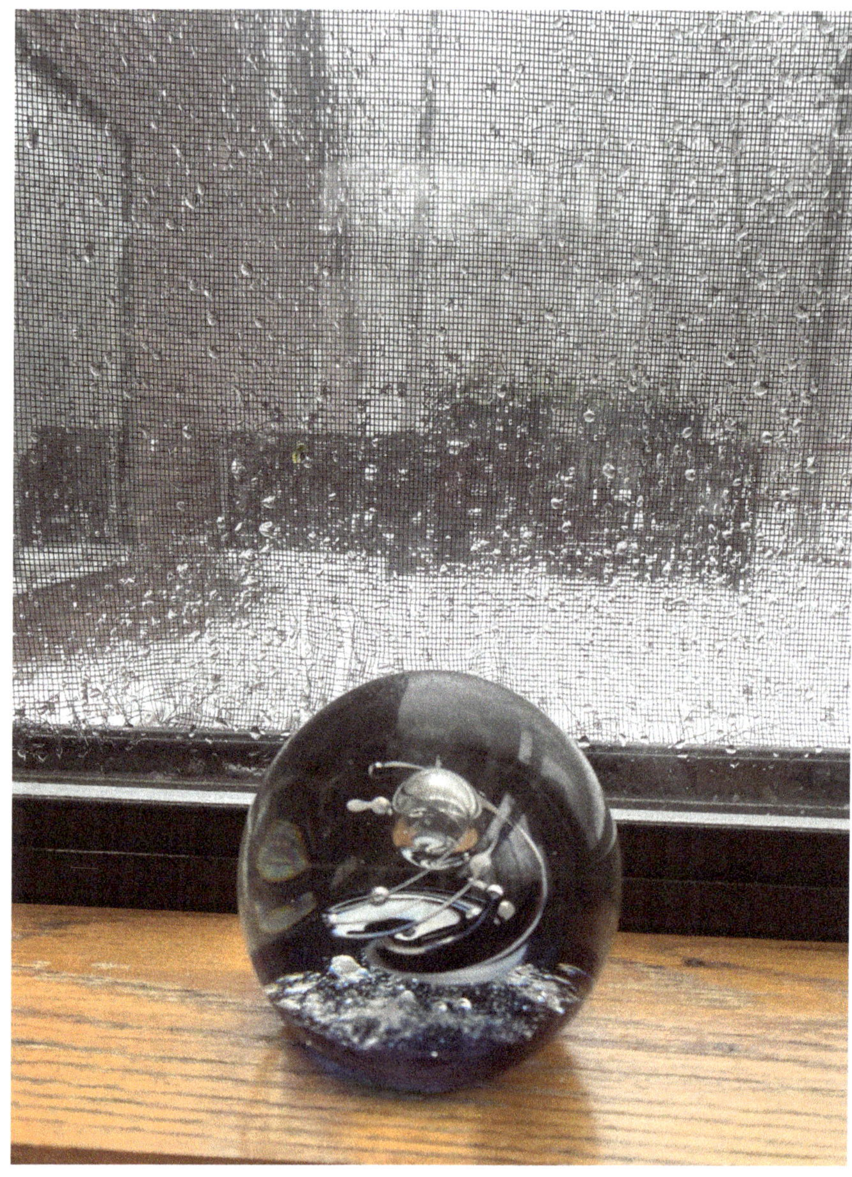

A whole world is within,
inseparable
from the world outside.
Seamless
and
held.

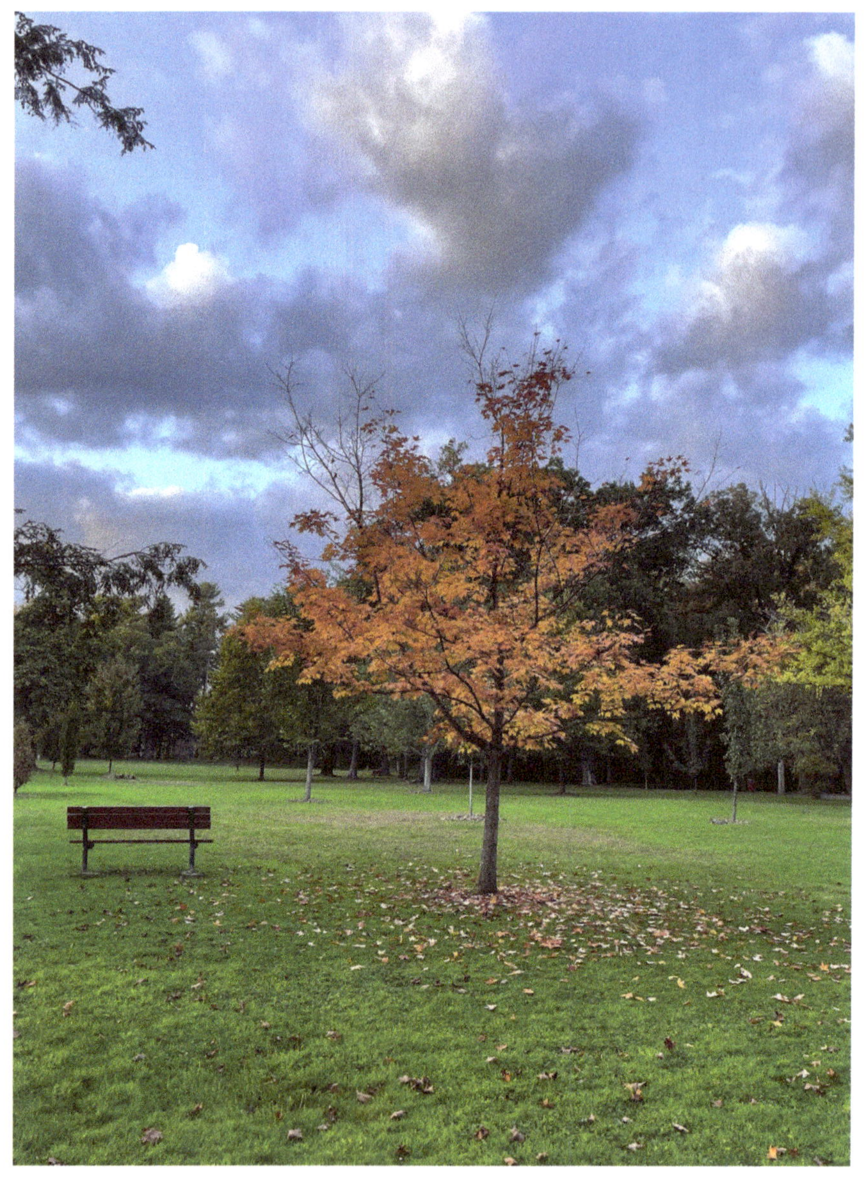

The work of meditation begins with
doing no harm.

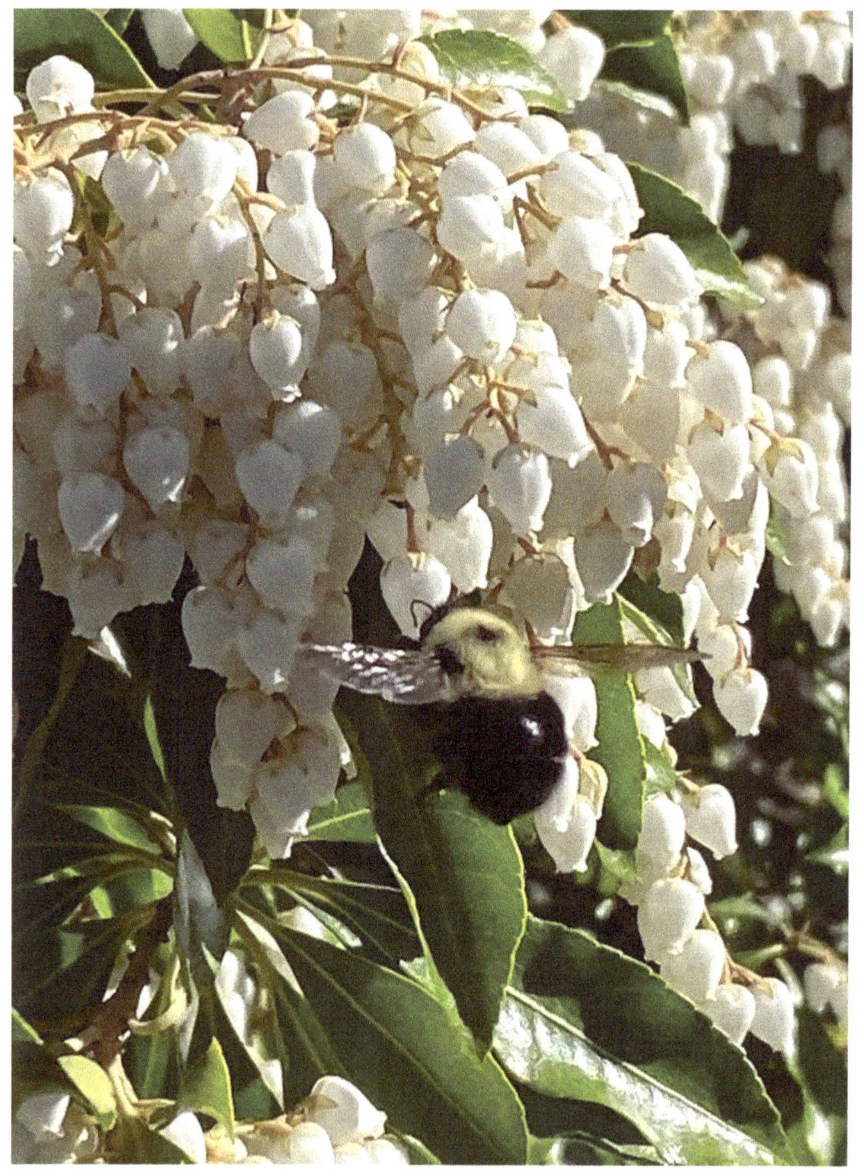

Make no mistake.
Everyone you meet

is

you.

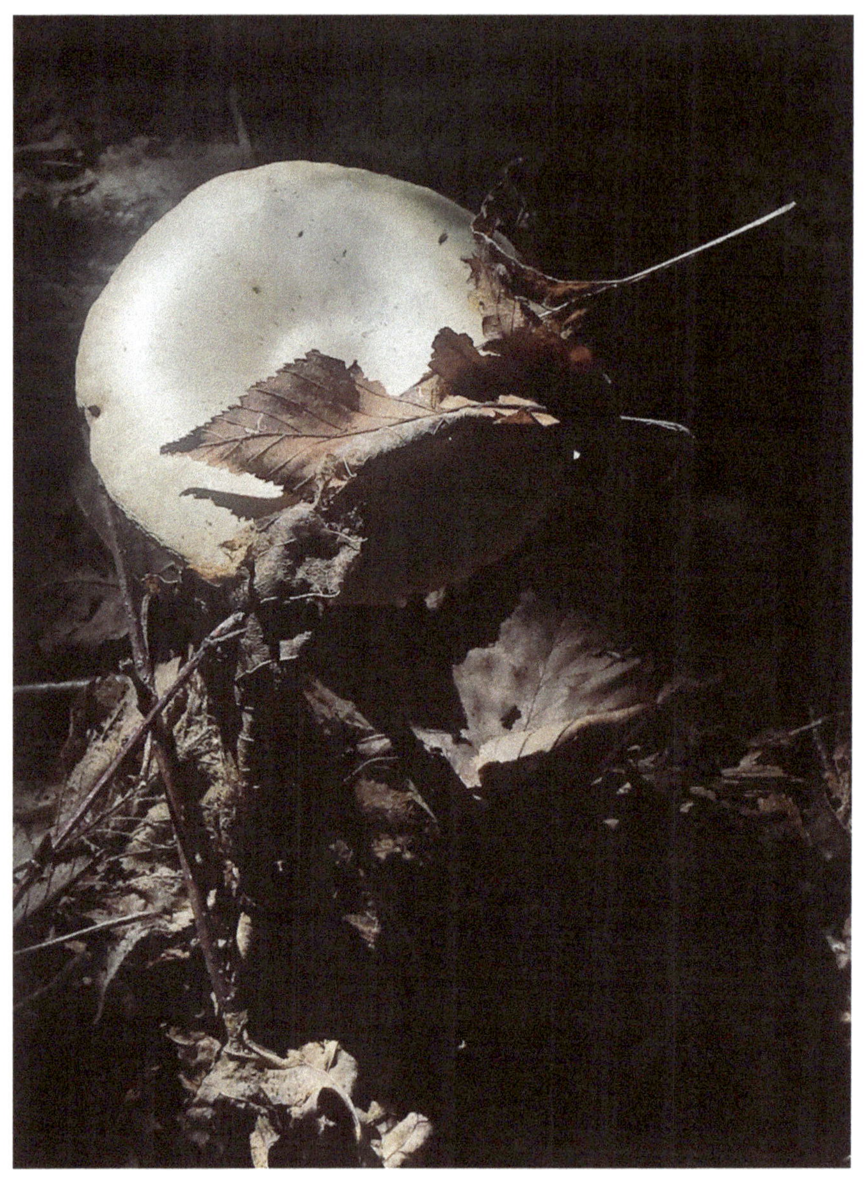

You extend far beyond,
farther than you can imagine.

We are One.

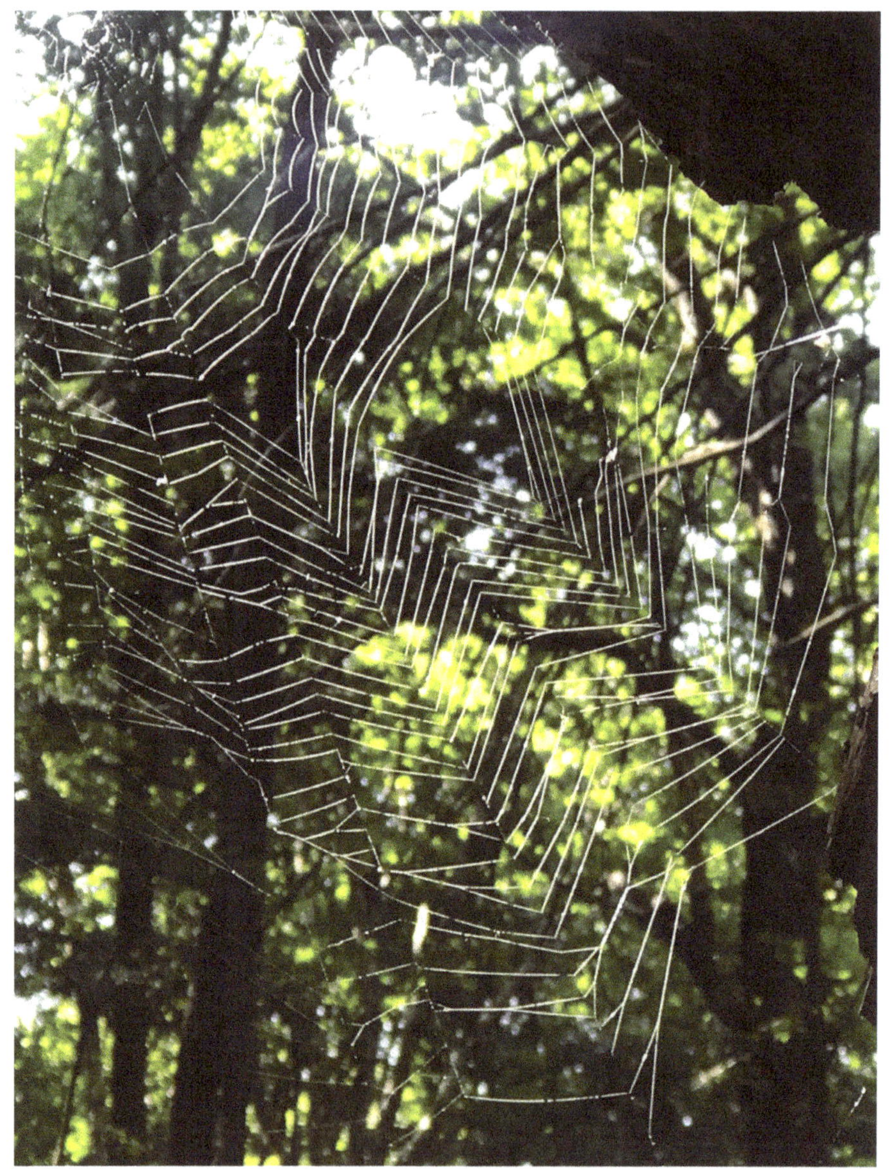

Sooner or later
we will go our separate ways.
But first,
realize we are not separate.

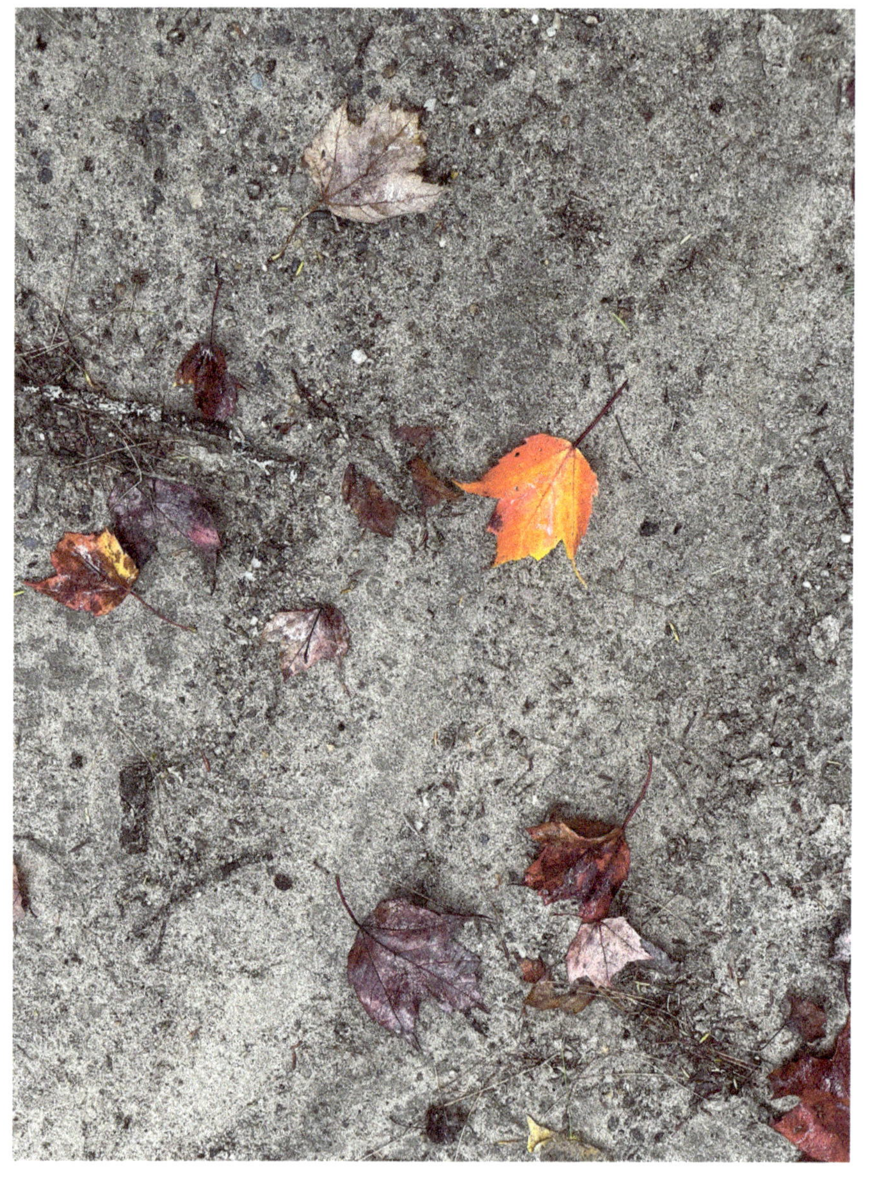

Our greatest challenge,
our greatest responsibility,
is to be with things
as they are.

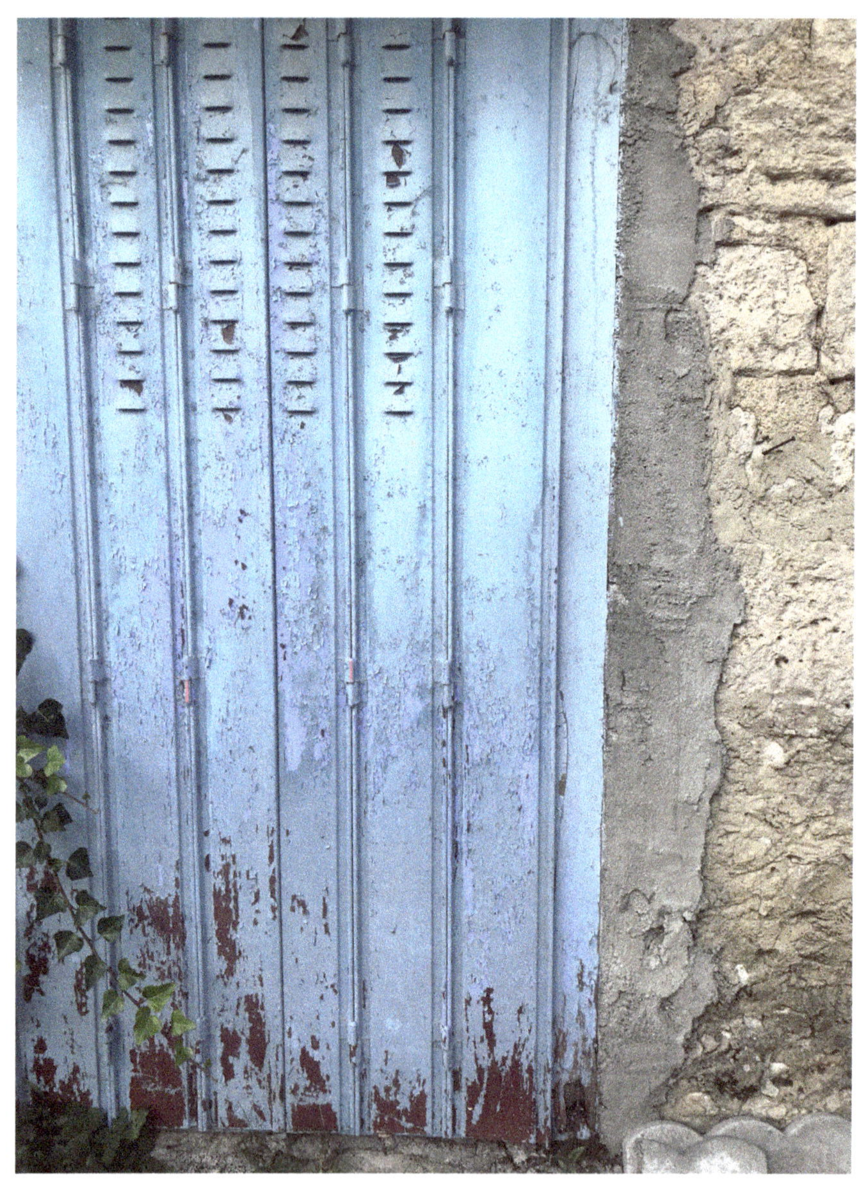

You do not have to try so hard
to keep things from falling apart.

Everything is made to
fall apart.

The mind will rest
when it opens
this
truth.

As we arise,
we pass away.

As we pass away,
we arise.

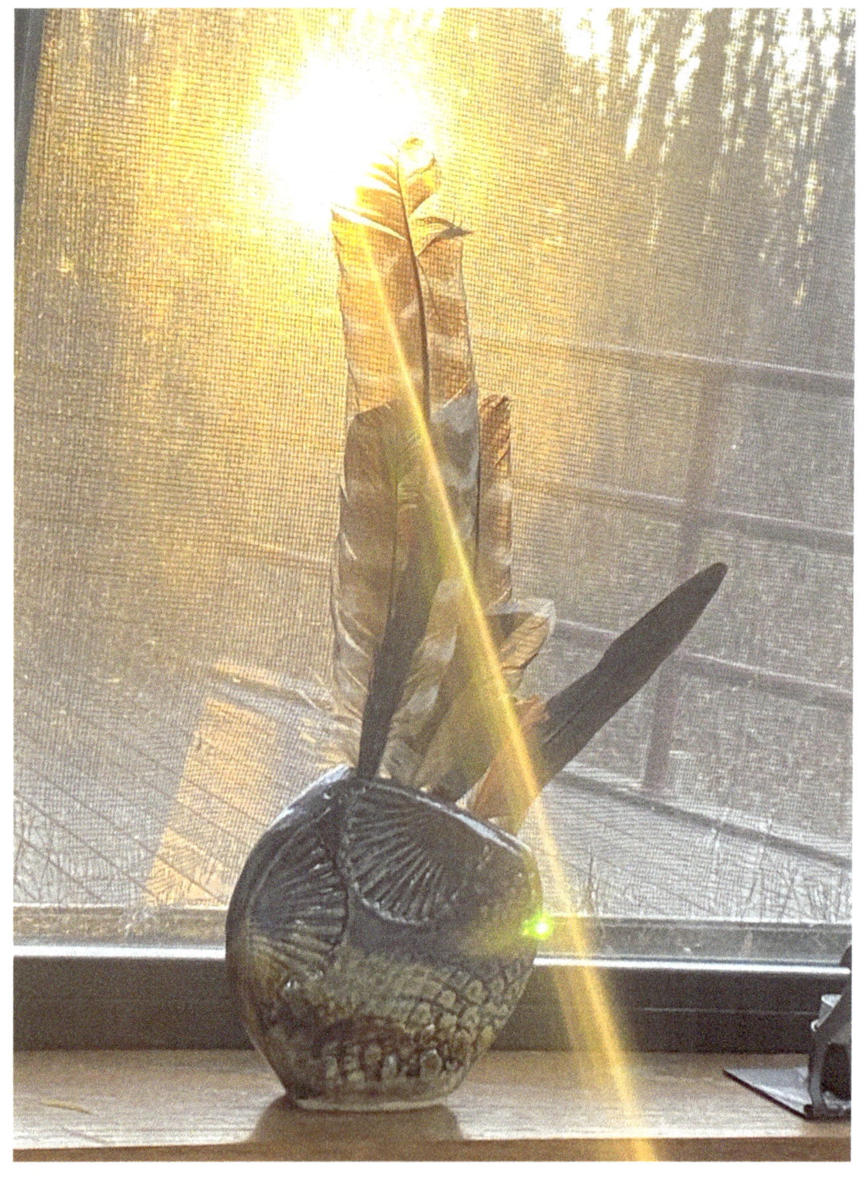

The happiness you long for
cannot be found outside yourself.
Turn inward.
Surrender.
Return.

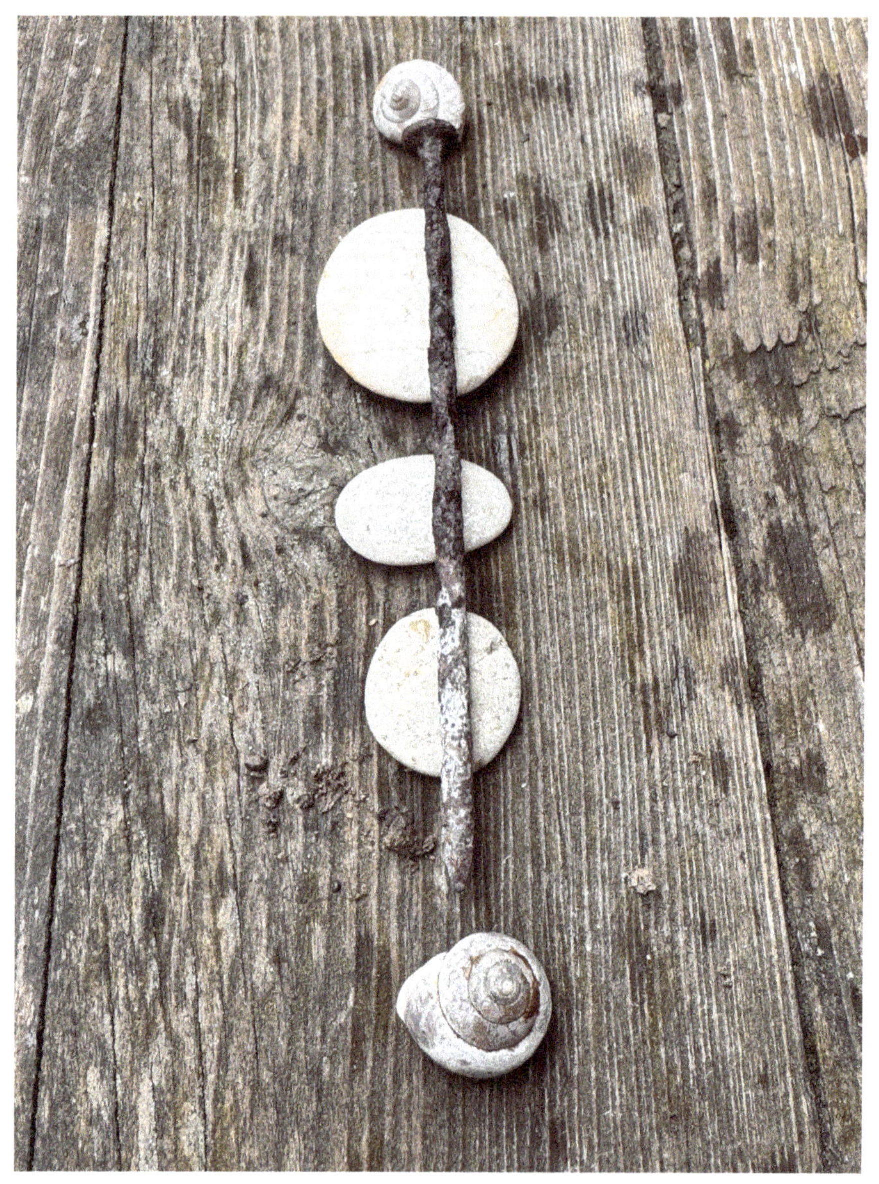

Sit with yourself as you are.
This touches your deepest longing.

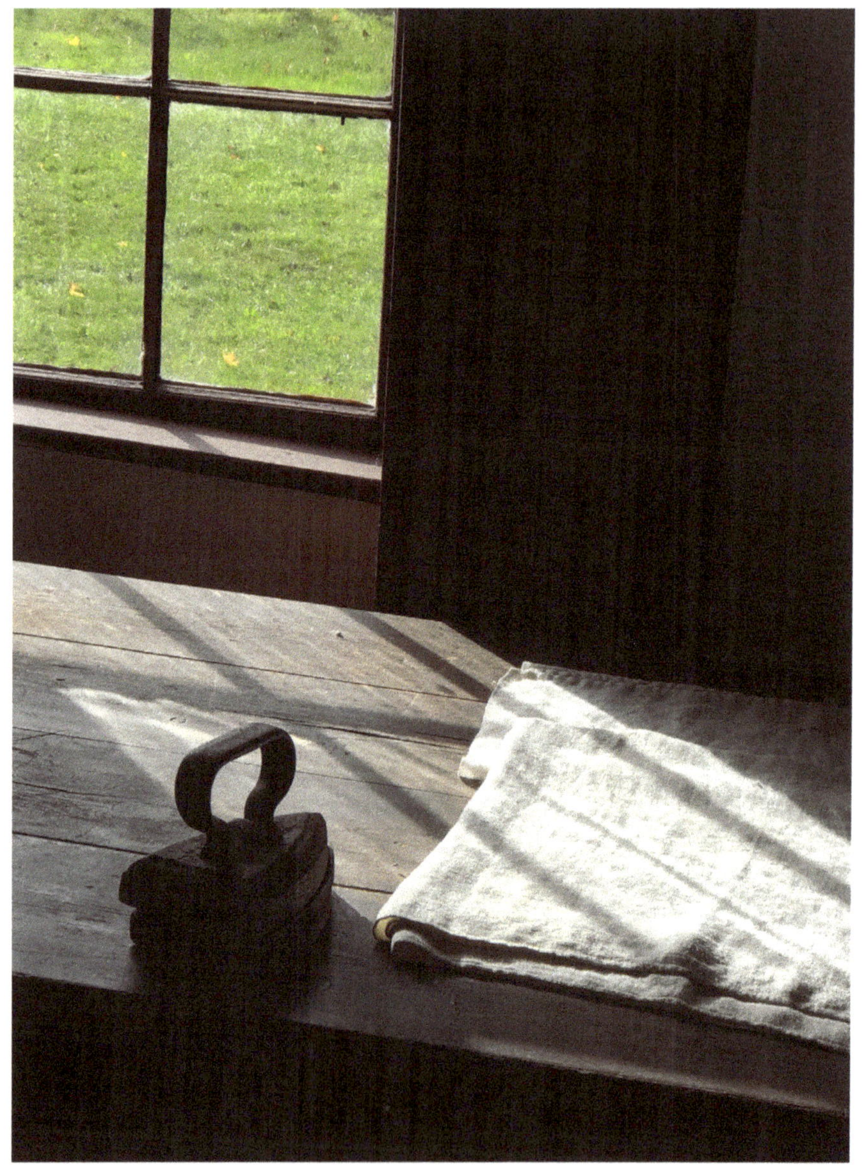

Take time to sit alone
and to be still.
Answers are born in silence,
which is not silent at all.

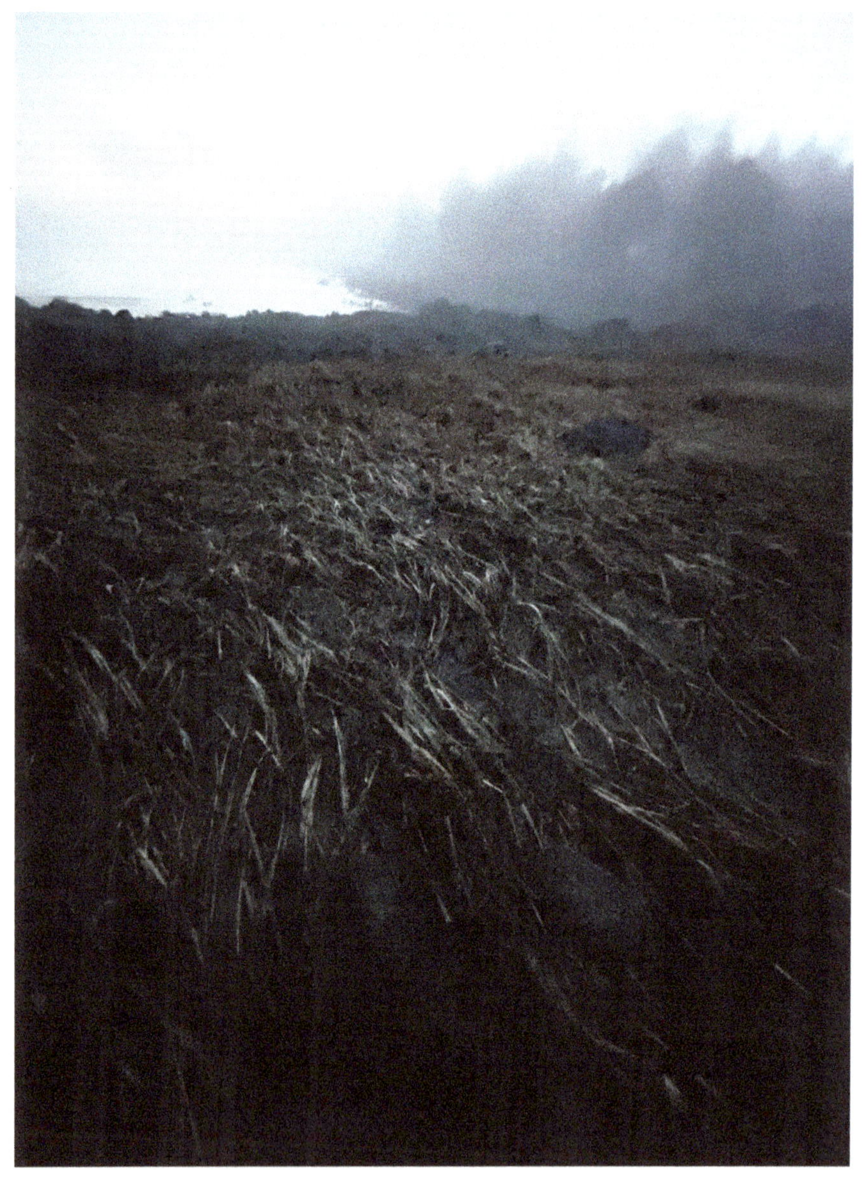

To meditate, plant your feet firmly on the ground.

Gather your courage.

Do not turn away.

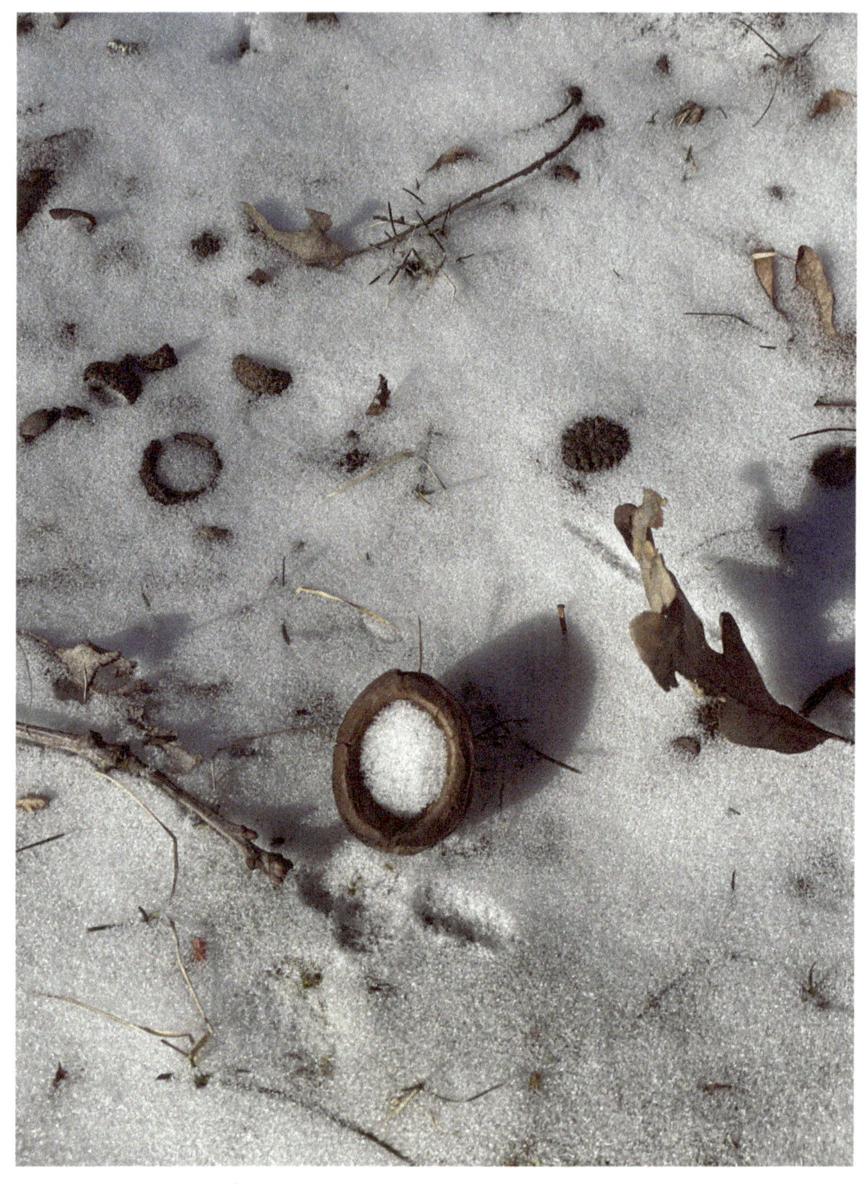

The path of practice will test you
again and again.

Only when you are at your breaking point,
can you break open.

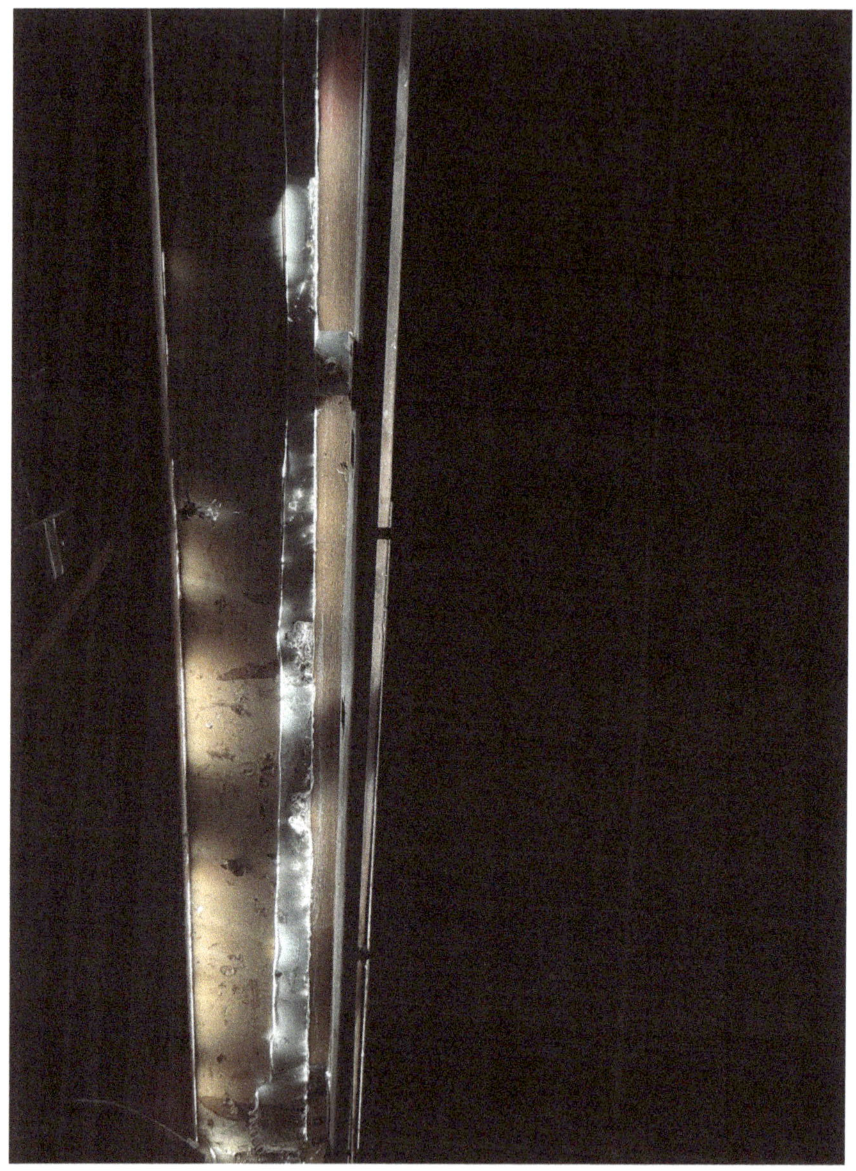

It is a difficult path.

Bring your rigor.

Bring your resolve.

Know the center of your suffering.

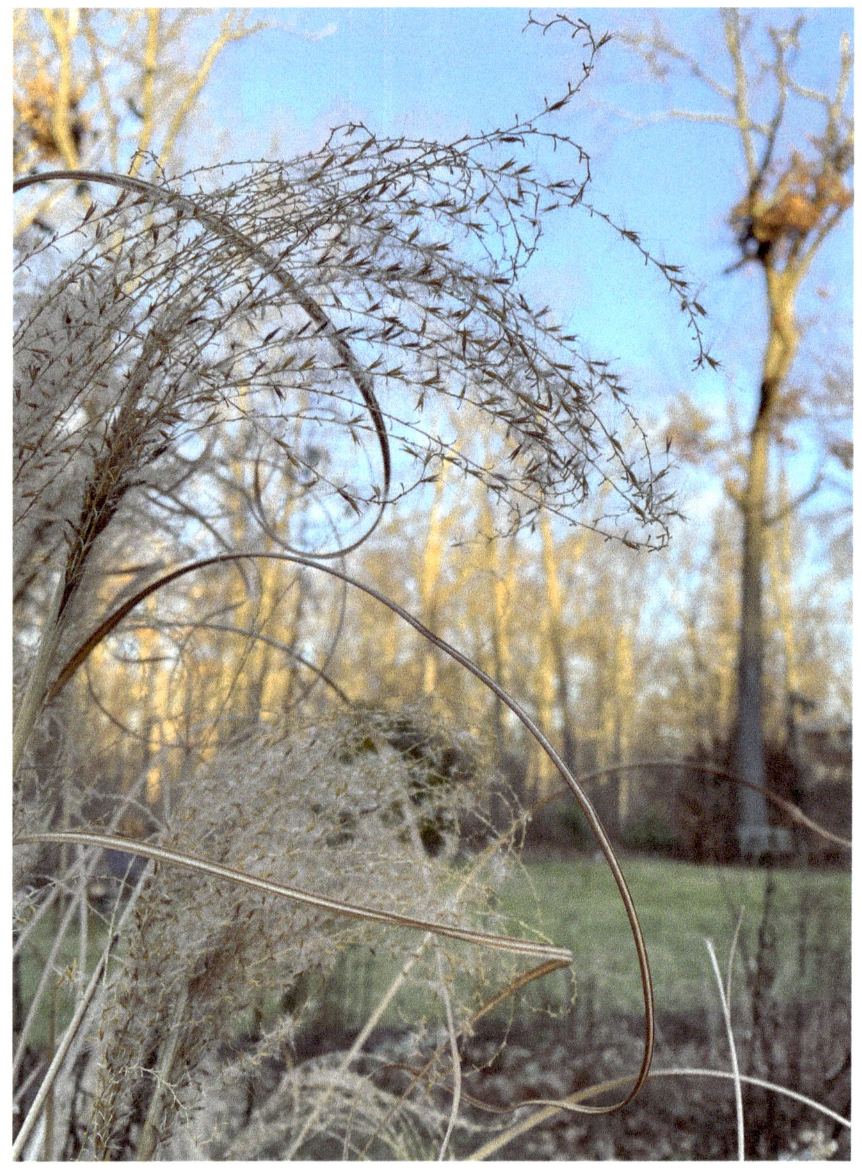

Patience.

Know each thread of your suffering
until it catches and begins
to unweave itself.

Surround each thread with compassion.

Freedom will follow.

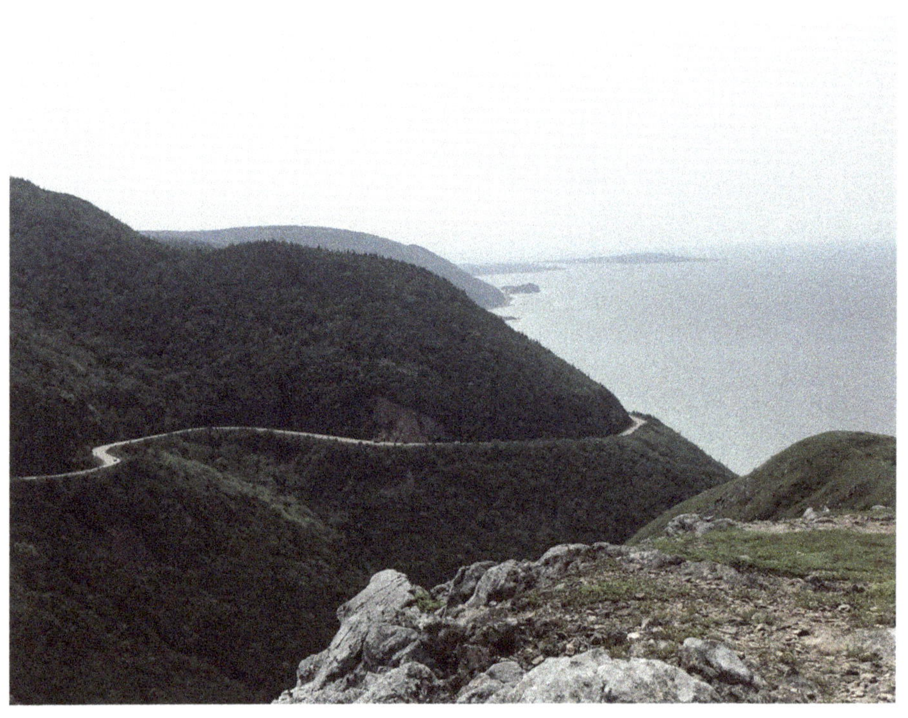

In the dense forest of my mind,
I was surprised to come
upon a
clearing
of
vast
stillness.
Looking back,
to realize
the forest was
an illusion.

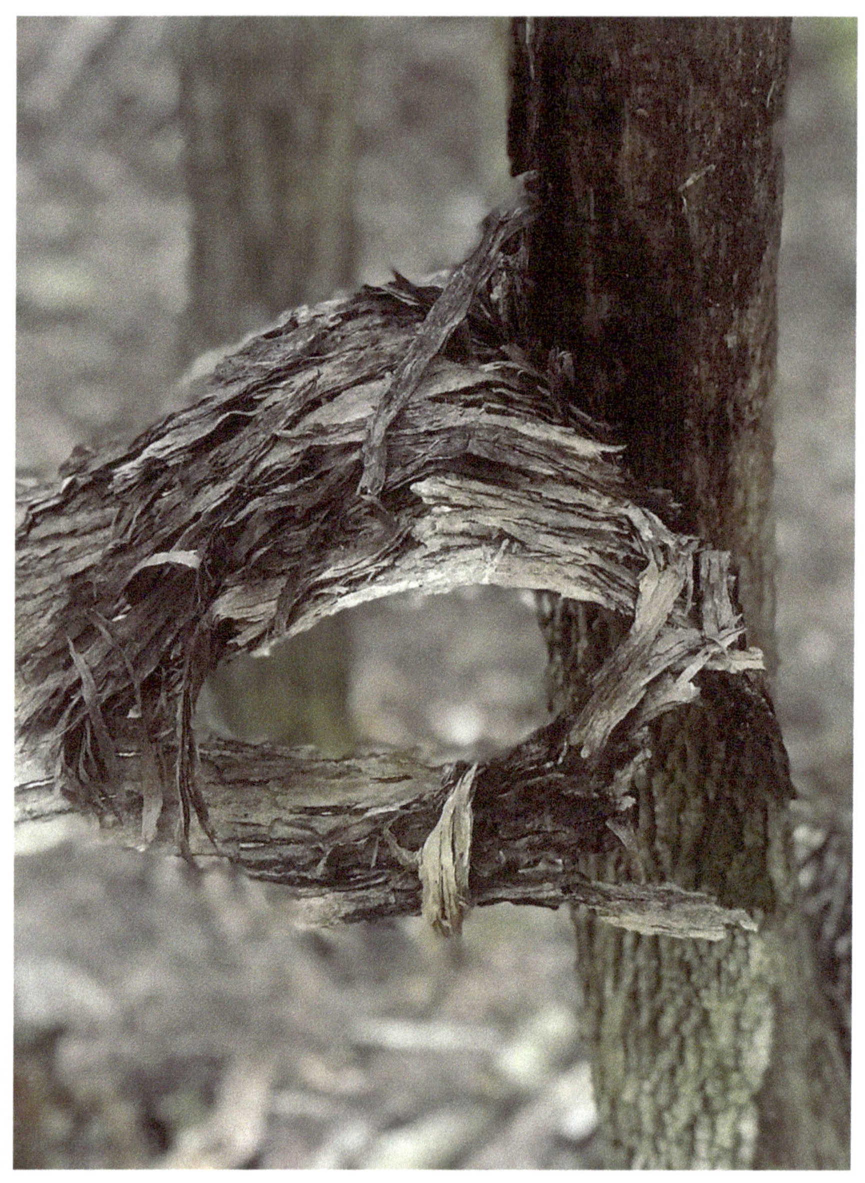

Peel away all the layers of your being,

each layer,

one

by

one.

Then peer inside.

Surprise!

Infinite, loving

Space.

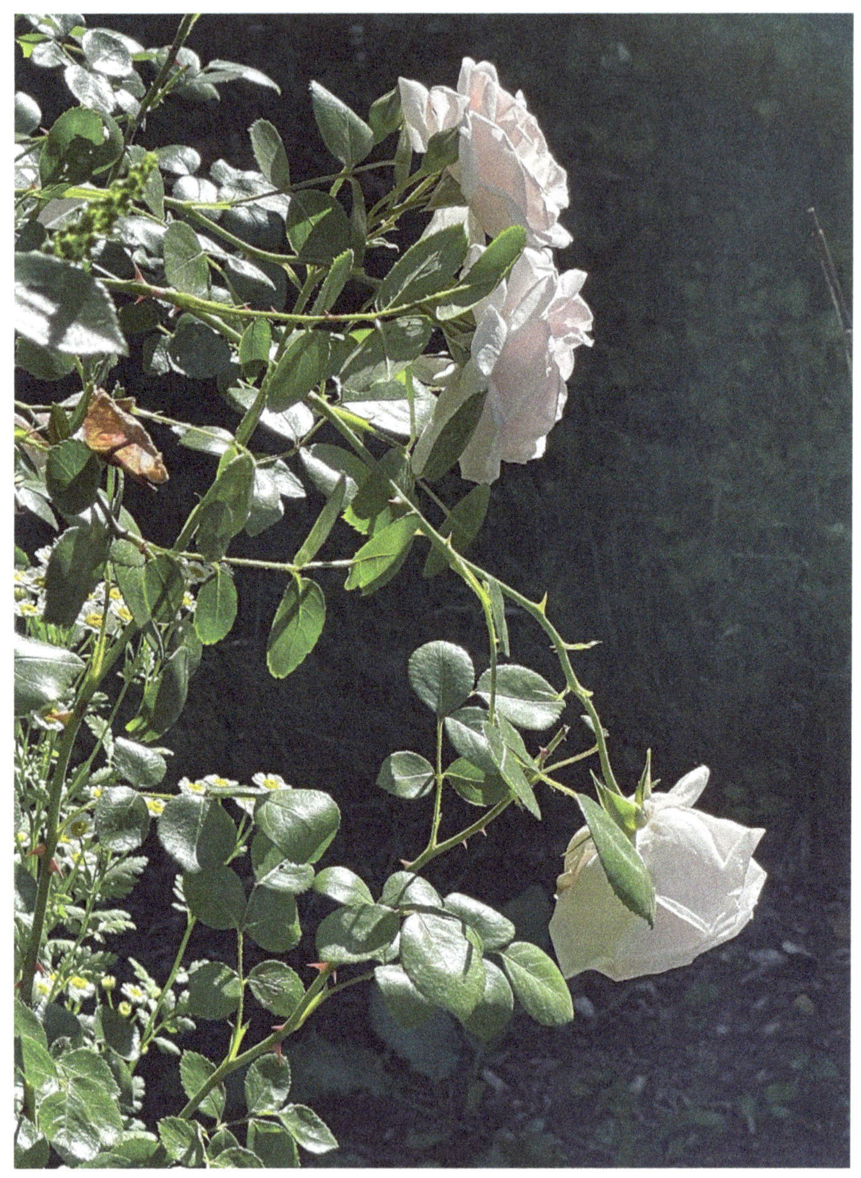

Let everything that happens surprise you.

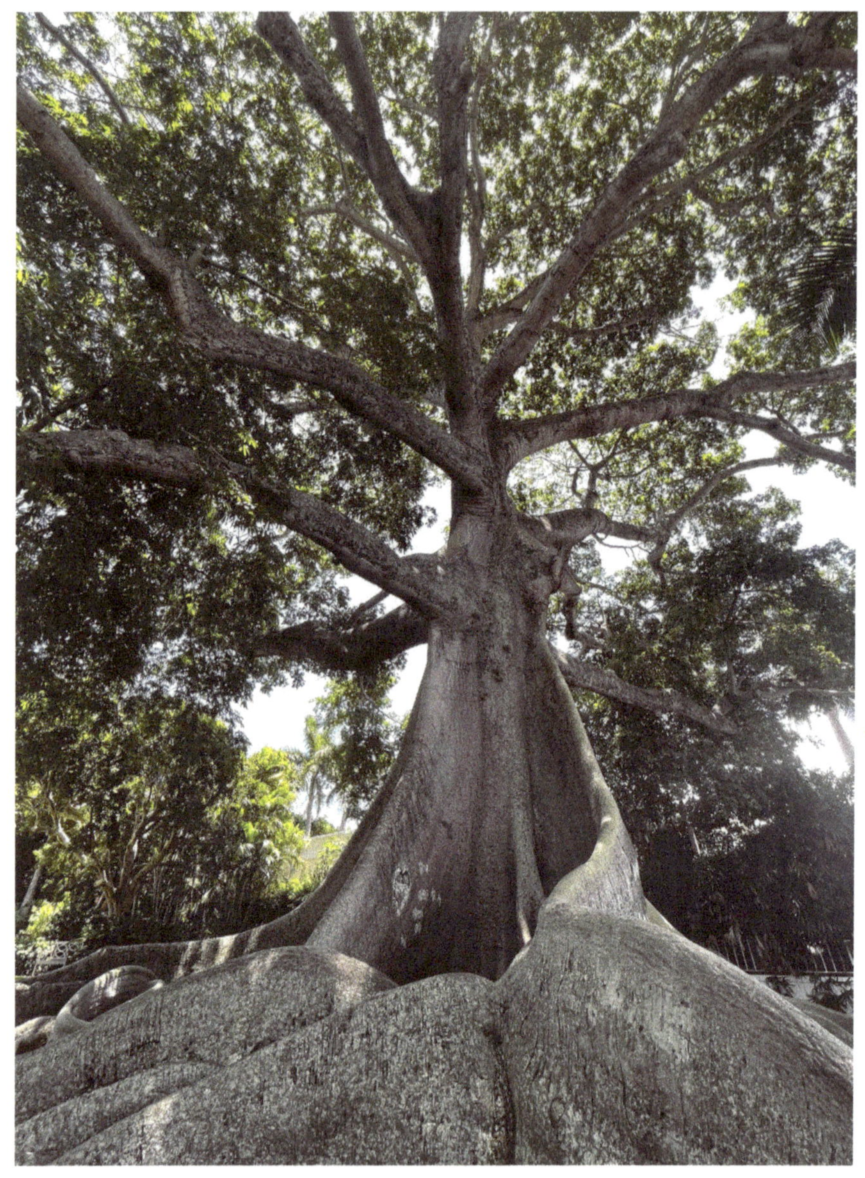

Look inside.
Much more awaits you here.
Stay a while.

An open sky will unveil itself.

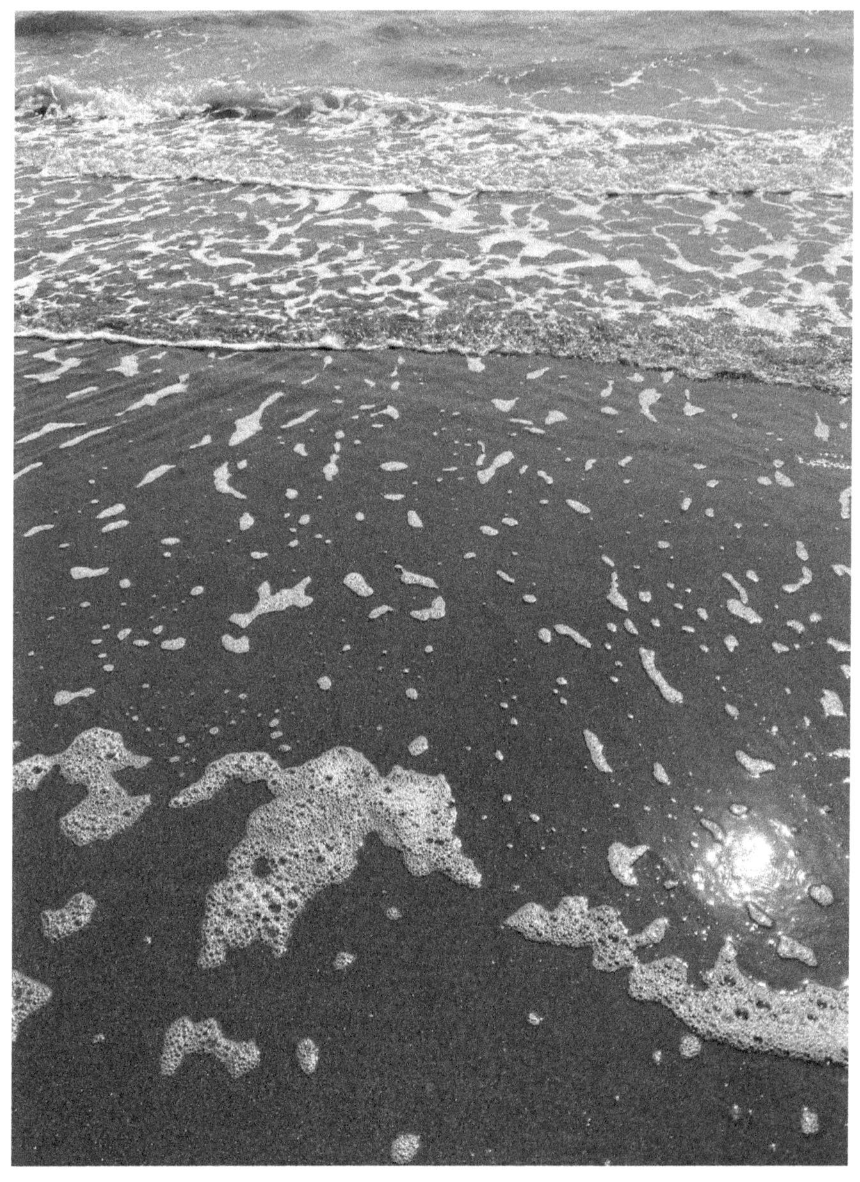

Each thought is birthed from Space
and returns to Space.

Watch the mind let go.

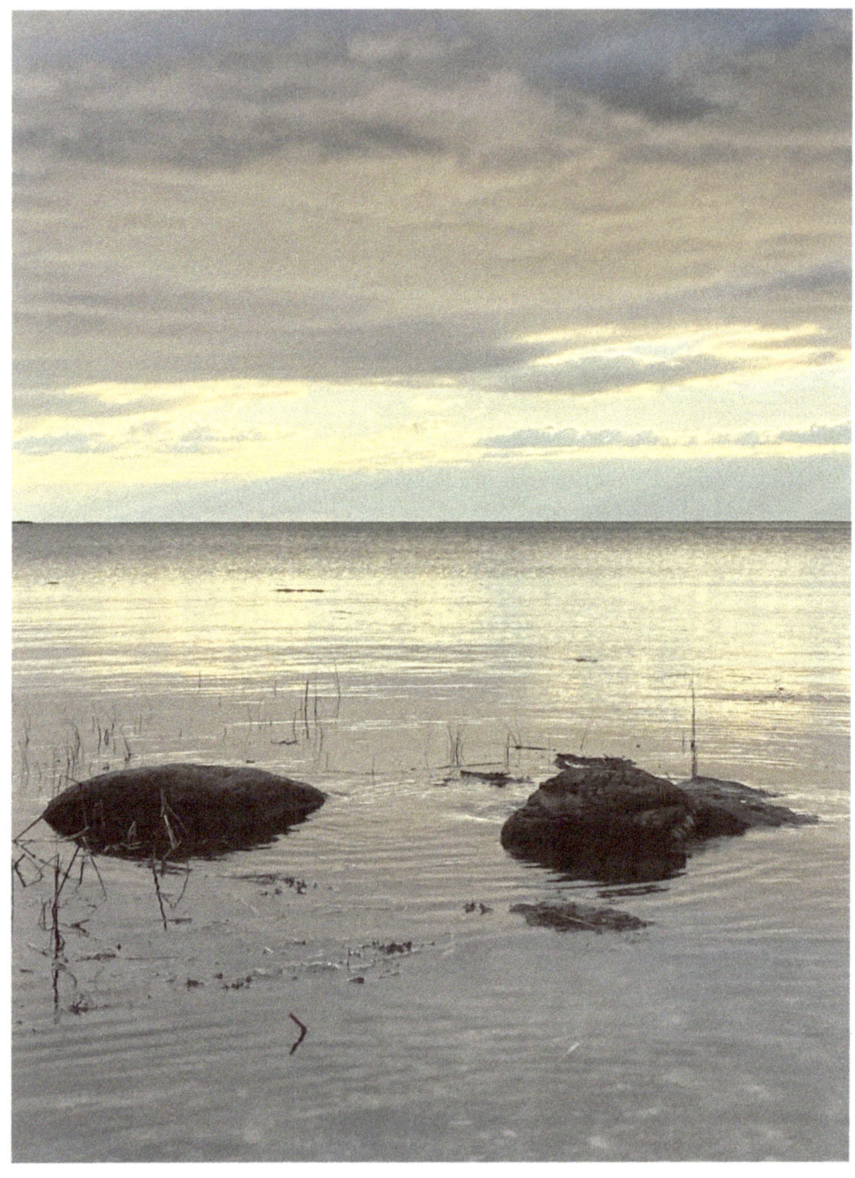

Dare to release the clinging mind of who you think you are.

Then listen.

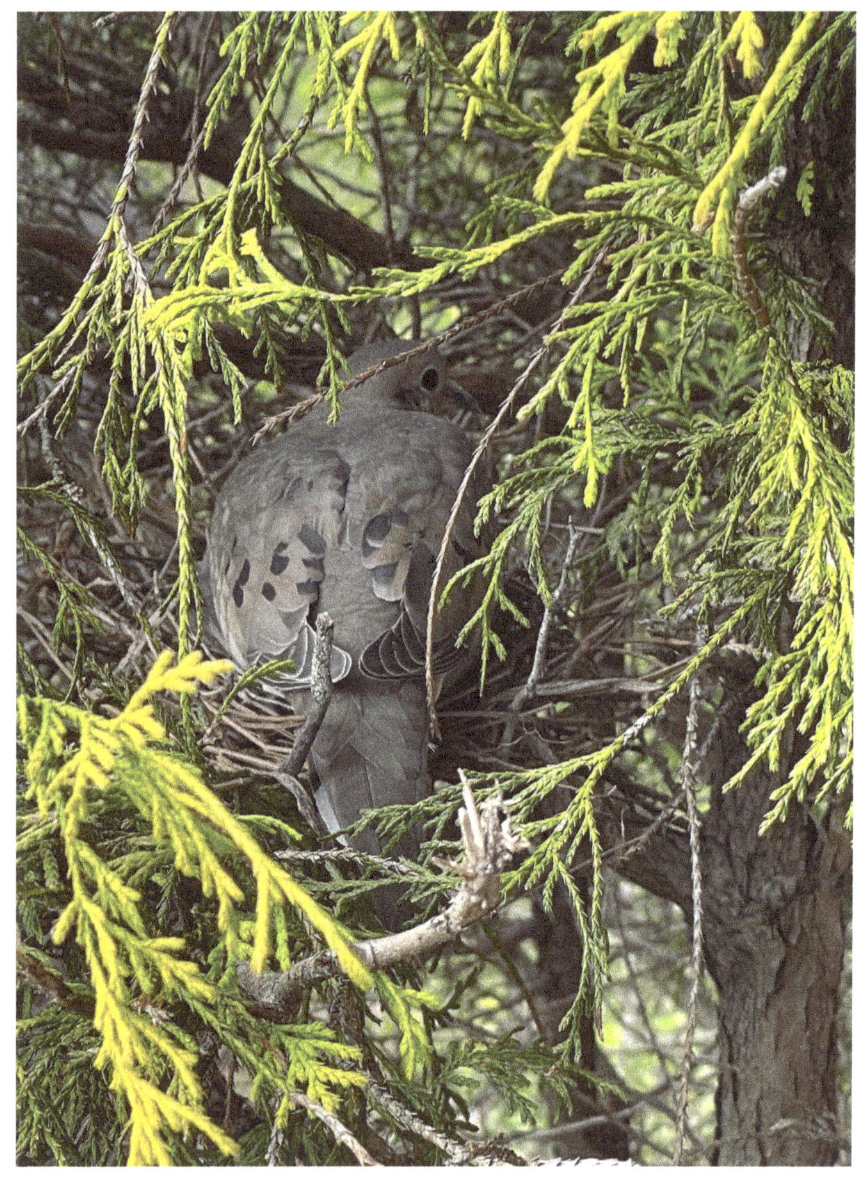

How do you set yourself free?

By realizing this:

There is no separate self to free.

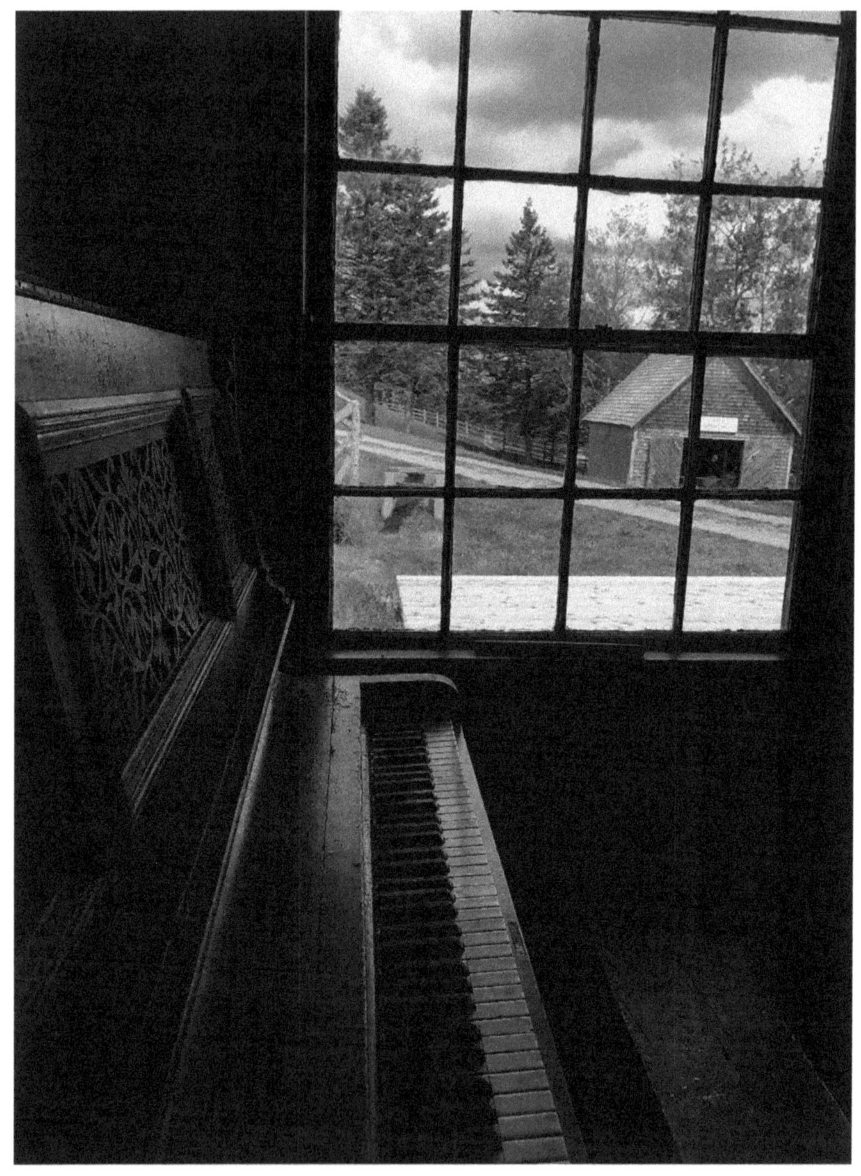

Once you have practiced the practice,
let the practice let go of you.

Embody this release.

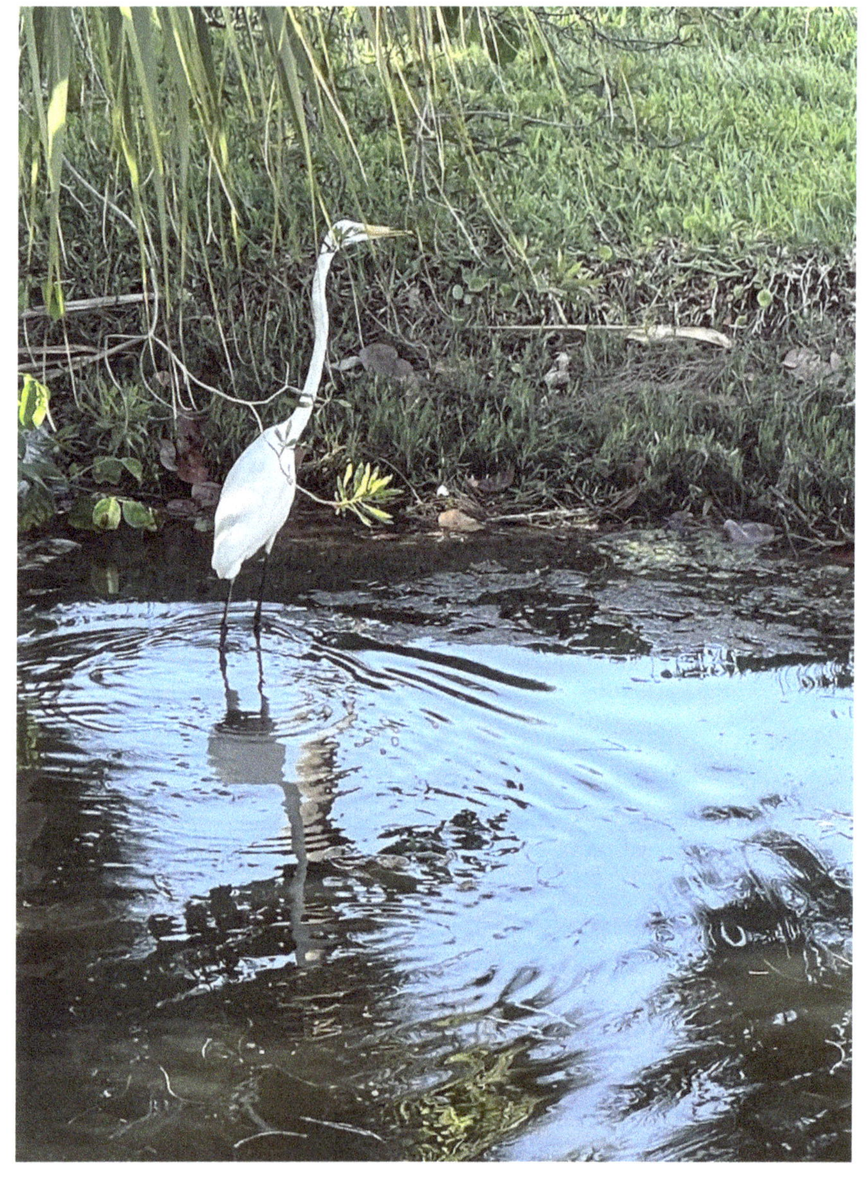

The setting sun and I merged
as the day died and the night gave rise.

The infinite sky within emerges.

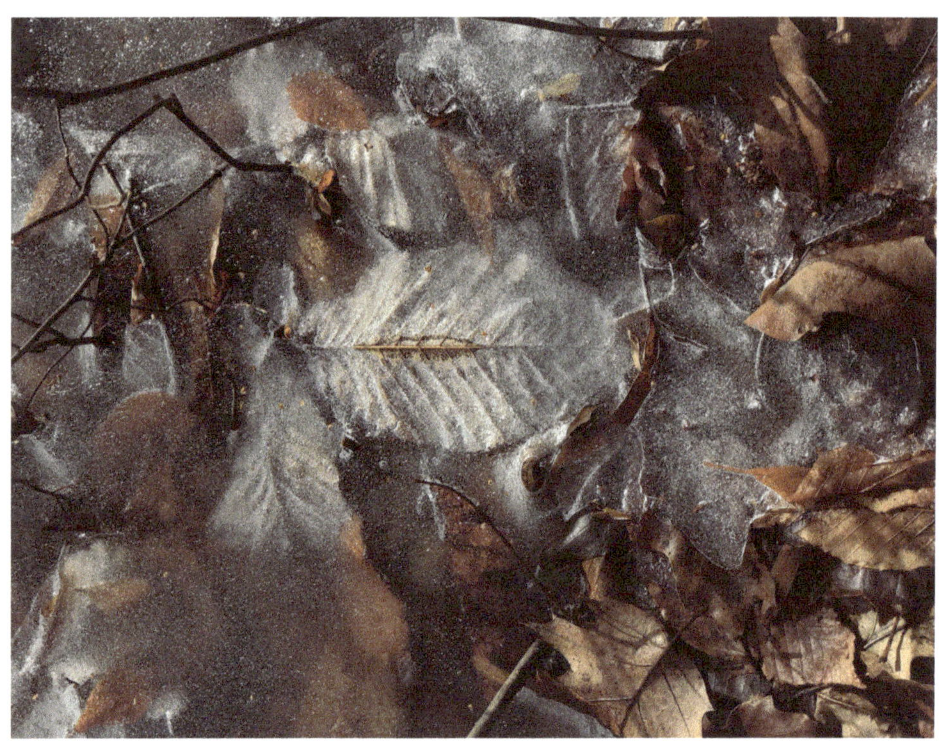

We

fall

fall

fall.

And then we

fall

away.

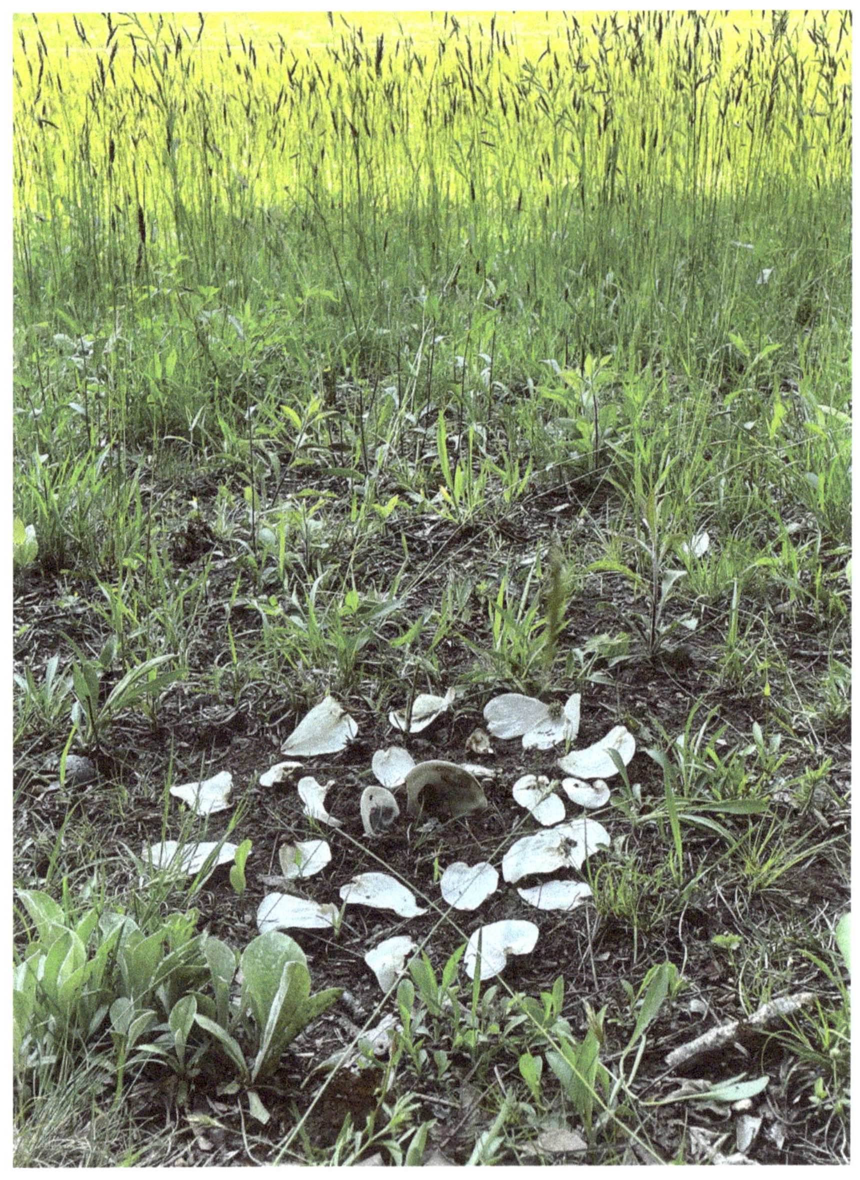

We think that birth is the beginning.
We think that death is the end.
Look deeply within.

Find that which is abiding.

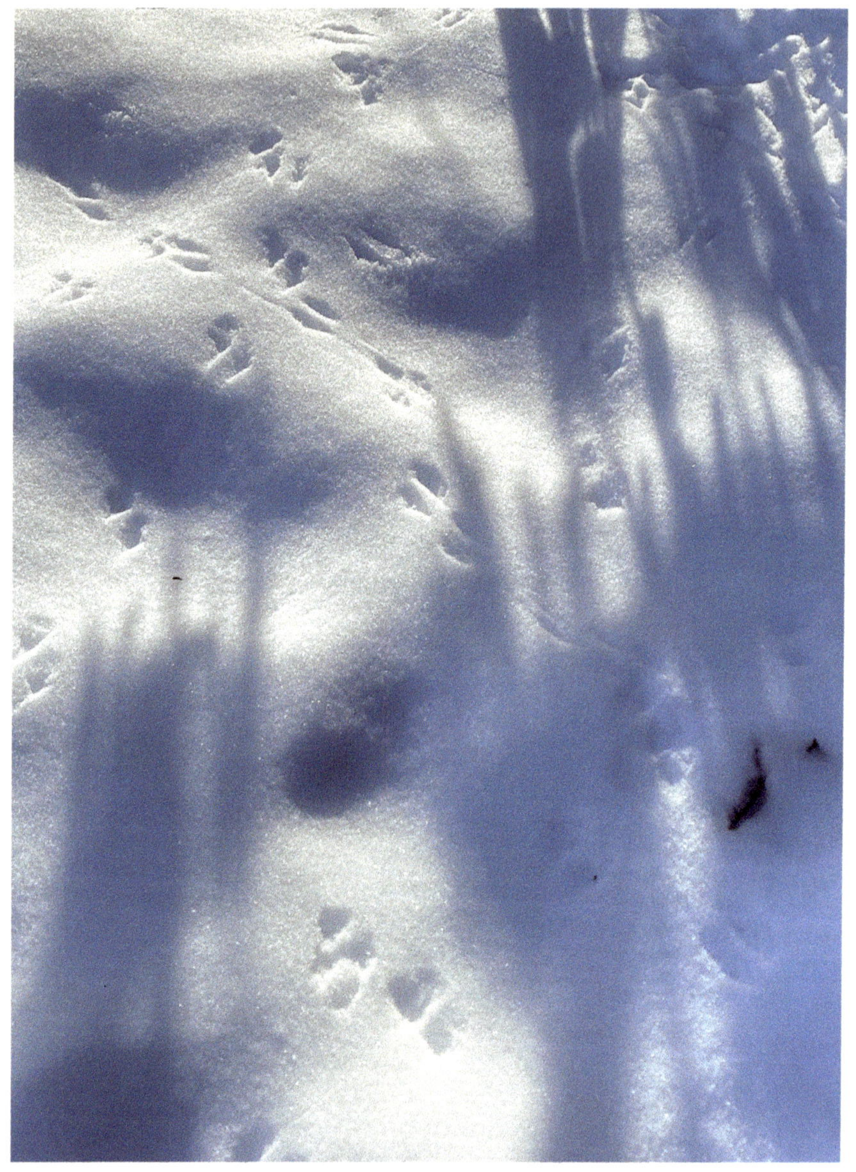

This beating heart,
these breathing lungs,
Nature decides.

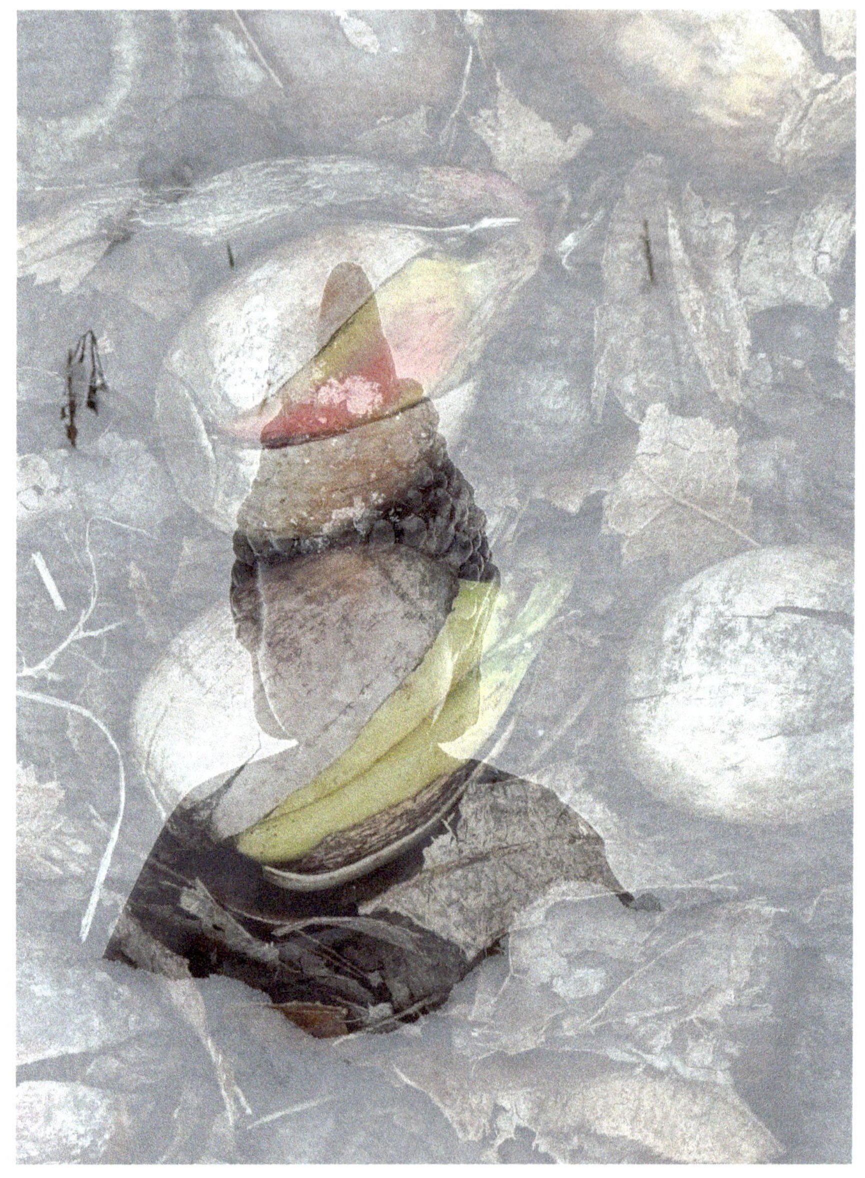

Where is the past?

Where is the future?

Is there any time at all?

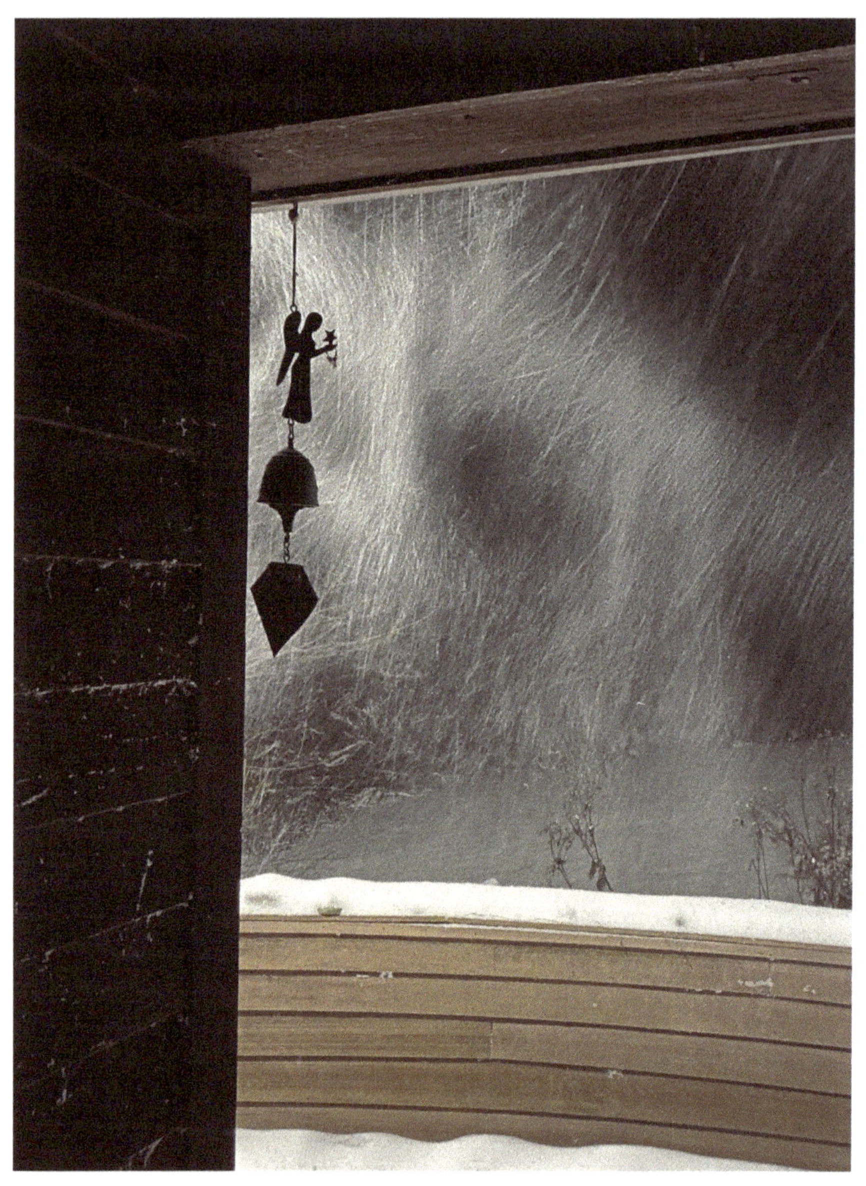

If Nature decides on snow, then it snows.

We fall
the way snow falls.

Snow neither plans its course of movement
nor protests its momentum.
Snow does not demand where the wind will carry it.
It gives Nature permission to cradle it,
to guide its soft landing
and then its melting
away.

Snow does not fear
its own vanishing
point.

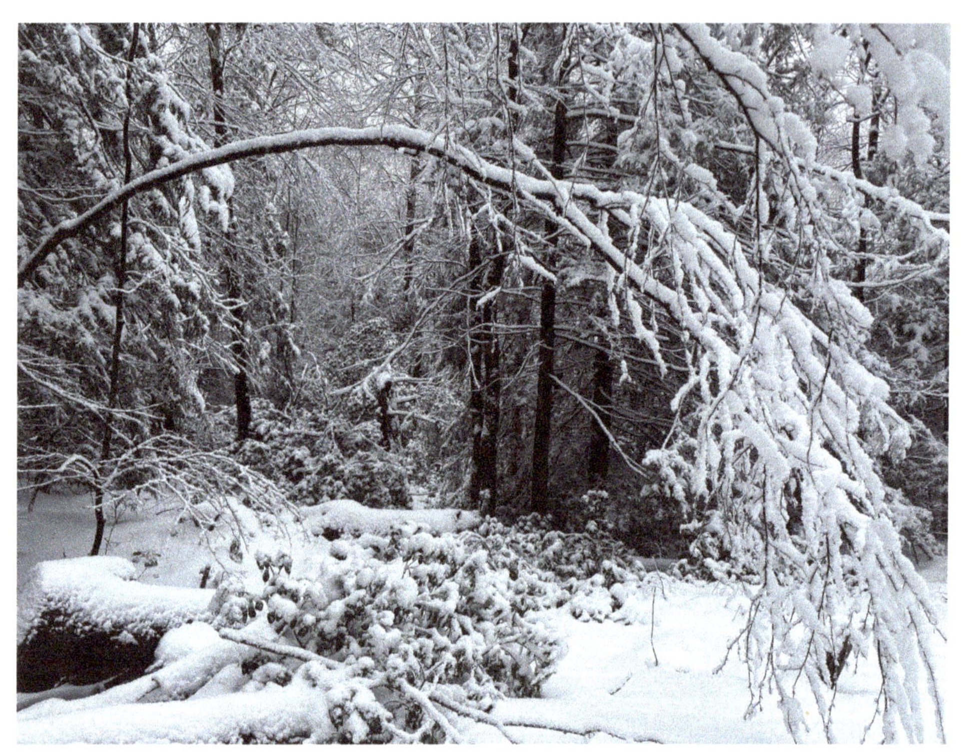

The life of snow
is
the free fall.

It knows no other way.

Like our life,
our fall is meant to happen.

This is Nature's way.

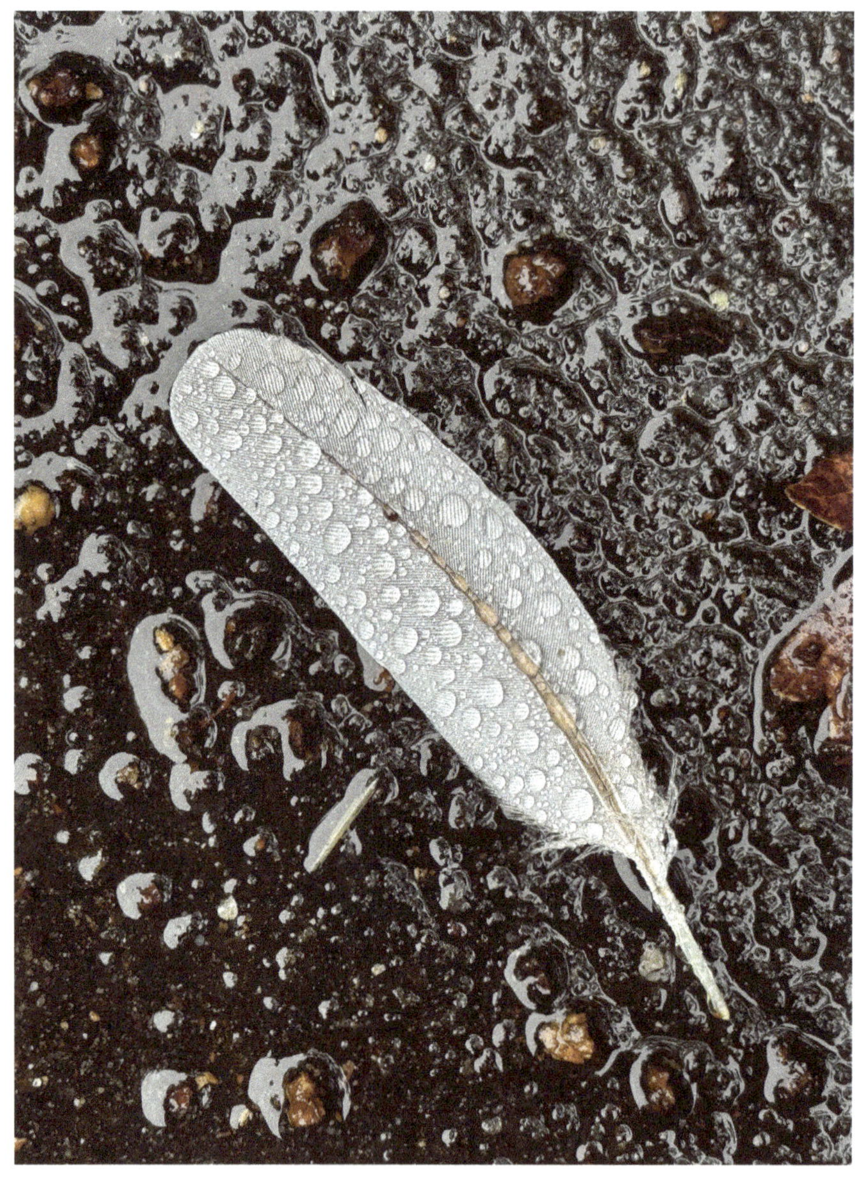

One day you will grow old.
Be still and gentle with this.
Hold this change.

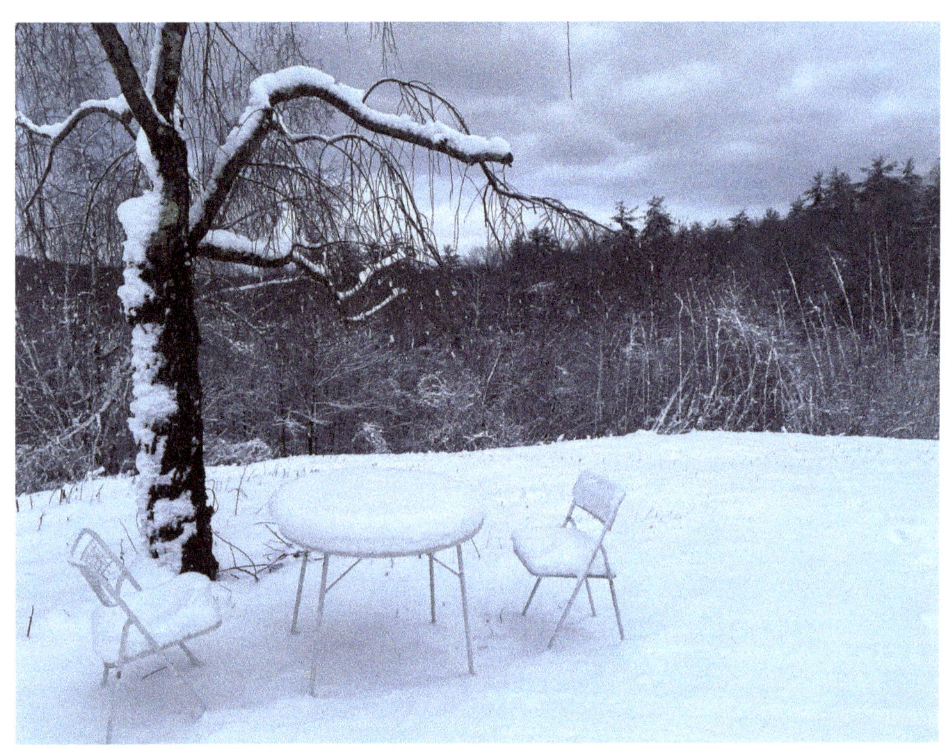

There is death.

There is no death.

At the same time,

and in no time at all.

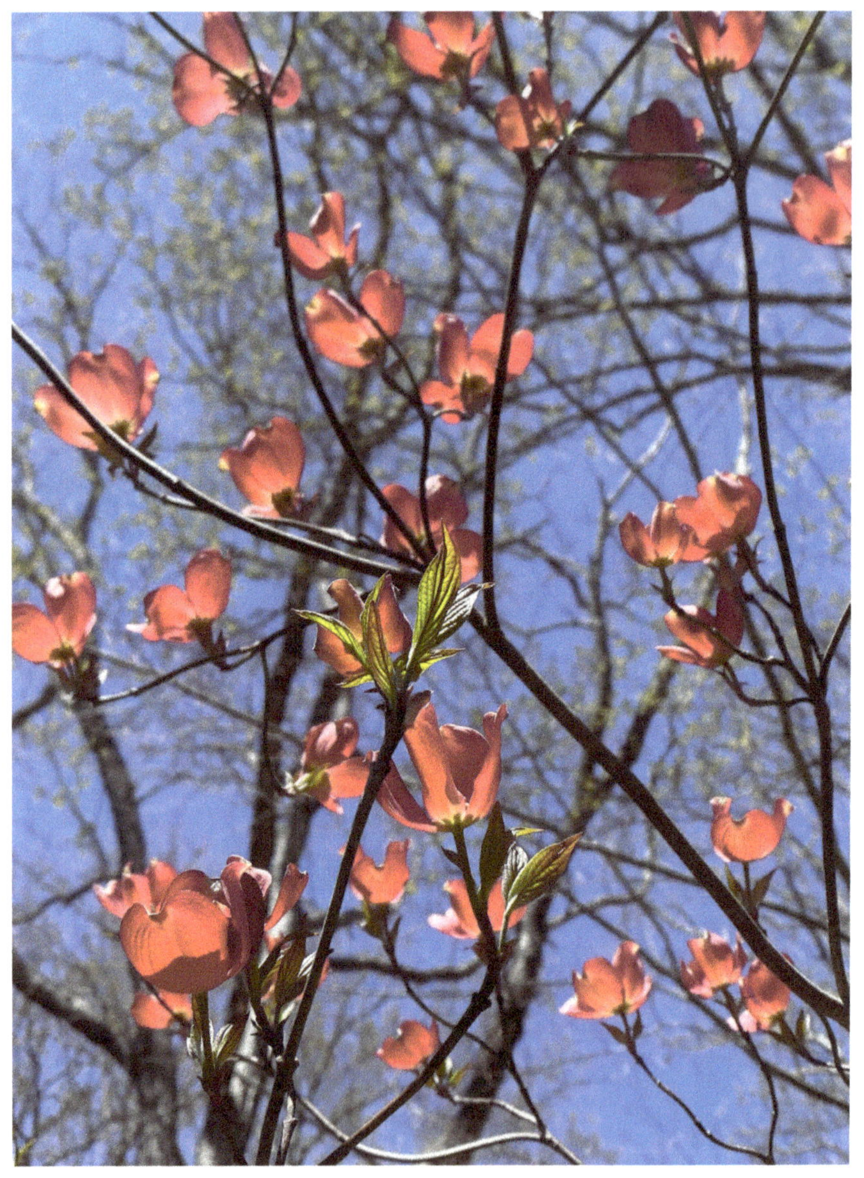

Where do the moments go?

Look closely.

See each moment
in the moment it passes away.

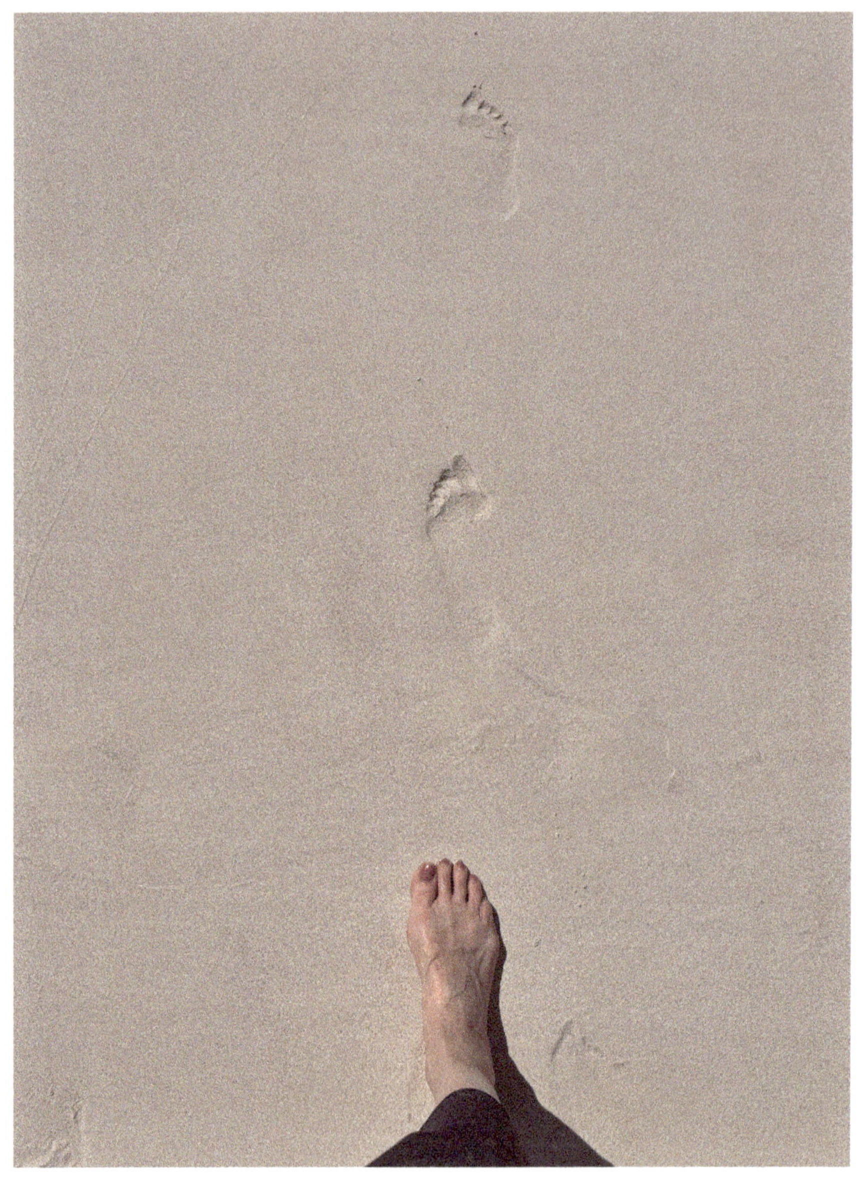

Why hold back?

The end is in sight.

The earth takes back its body
to begin again.

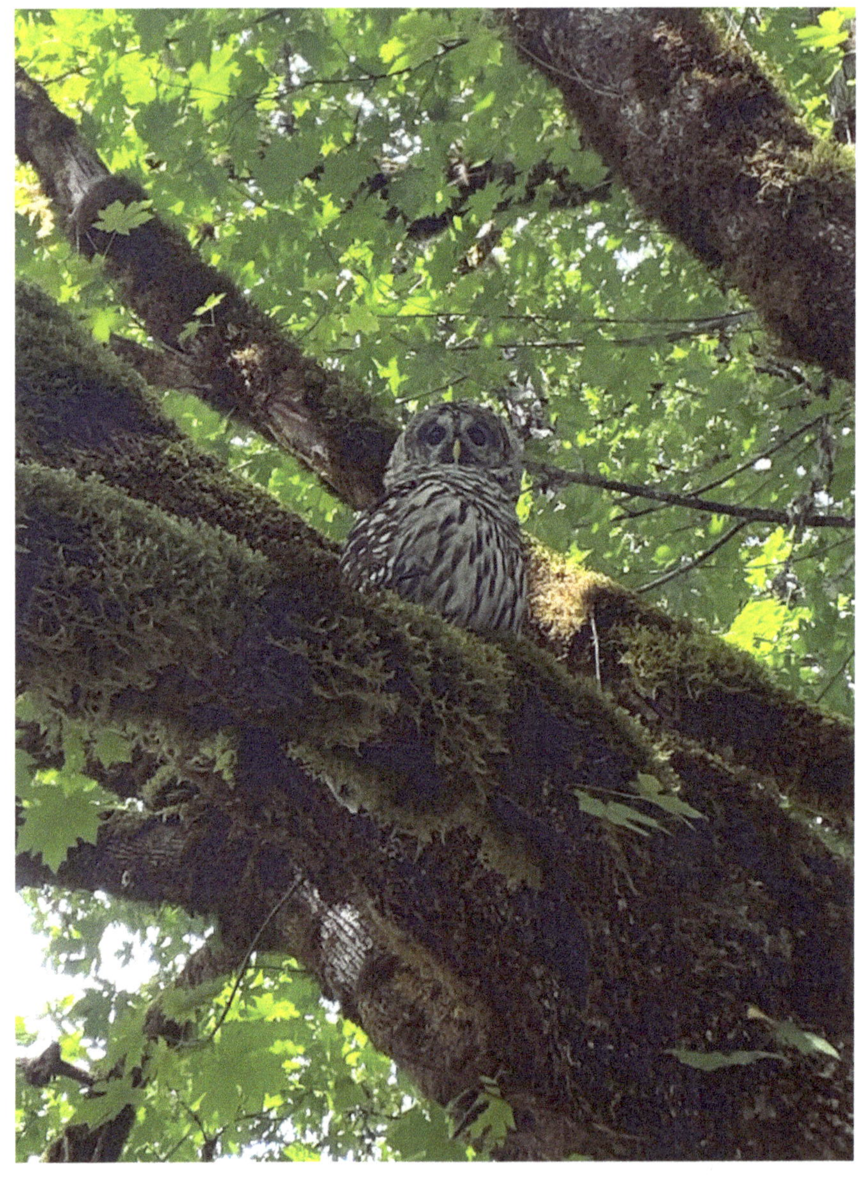

Death is always close by.

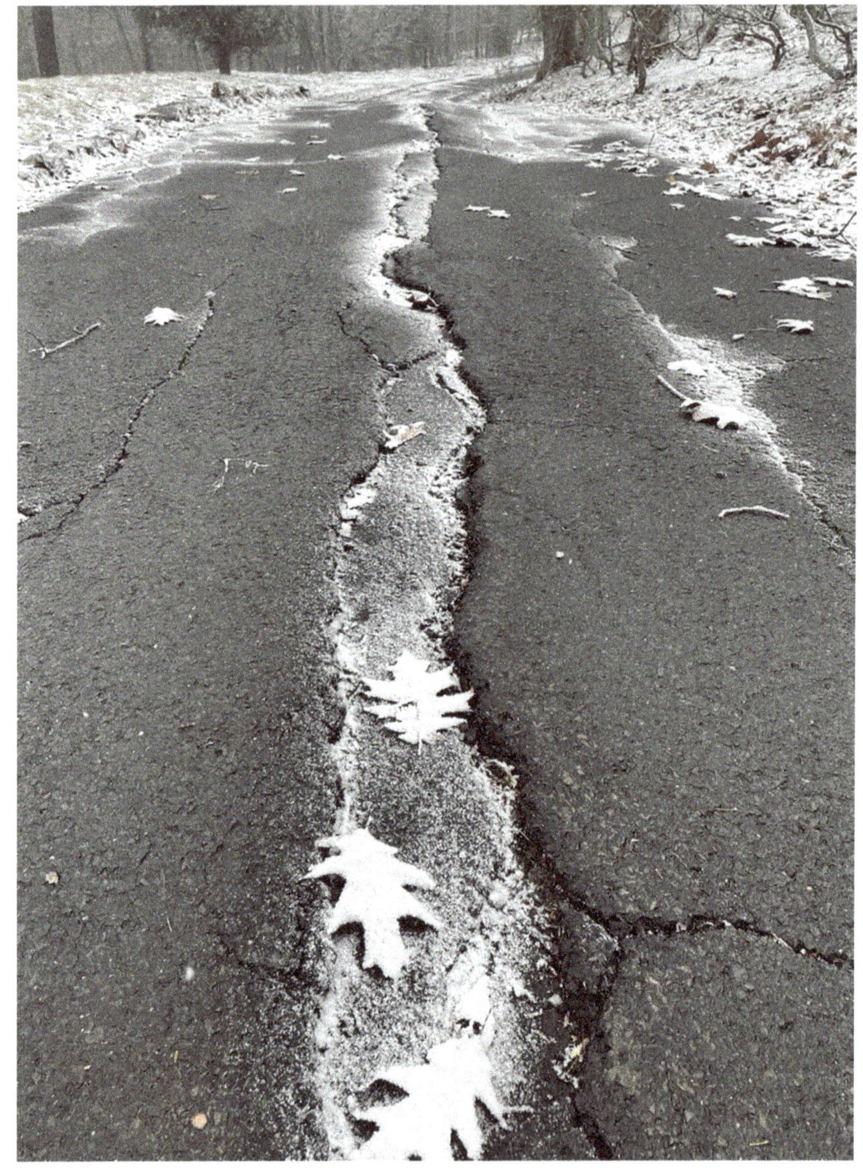

It is not up to you.

Love brought you here.

Love will take you back when it is your time.

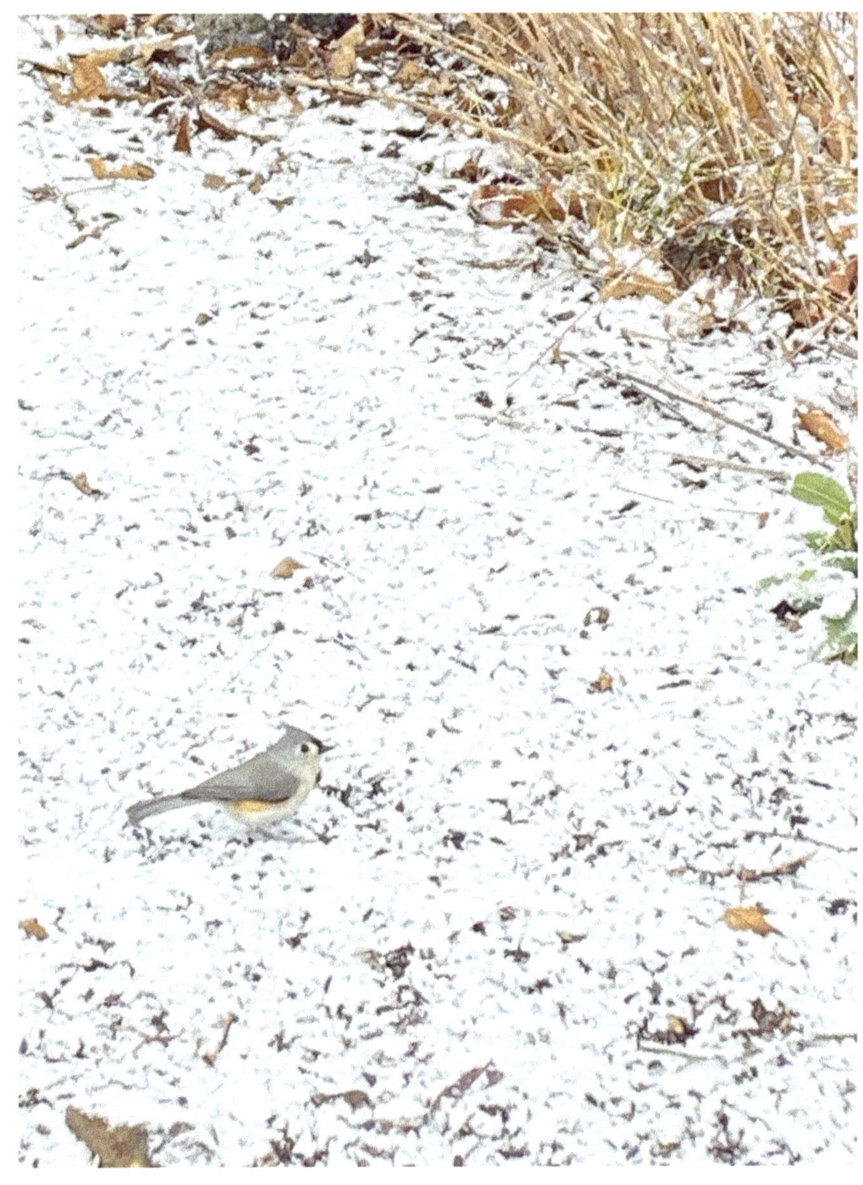

As we belong to life, so do we belong to death.

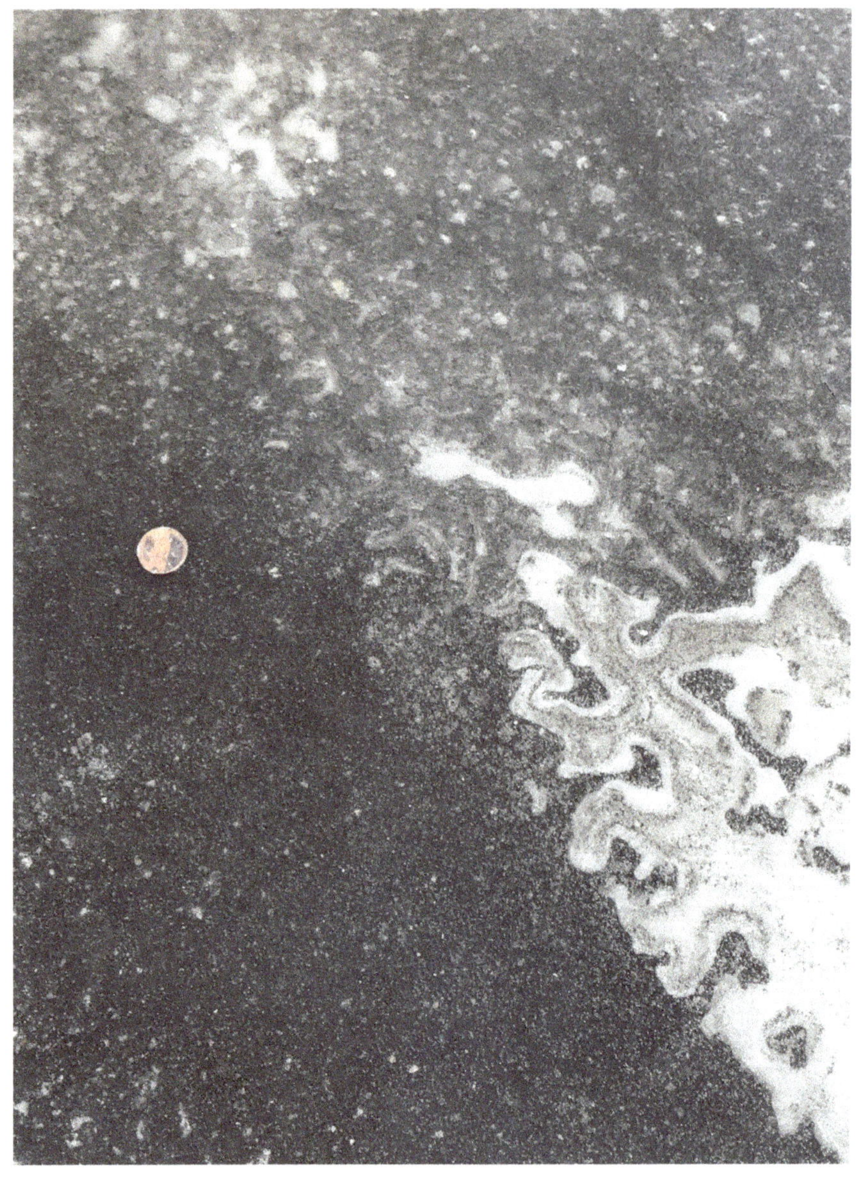

What is it like to not know
what will happen next?

Abide here.

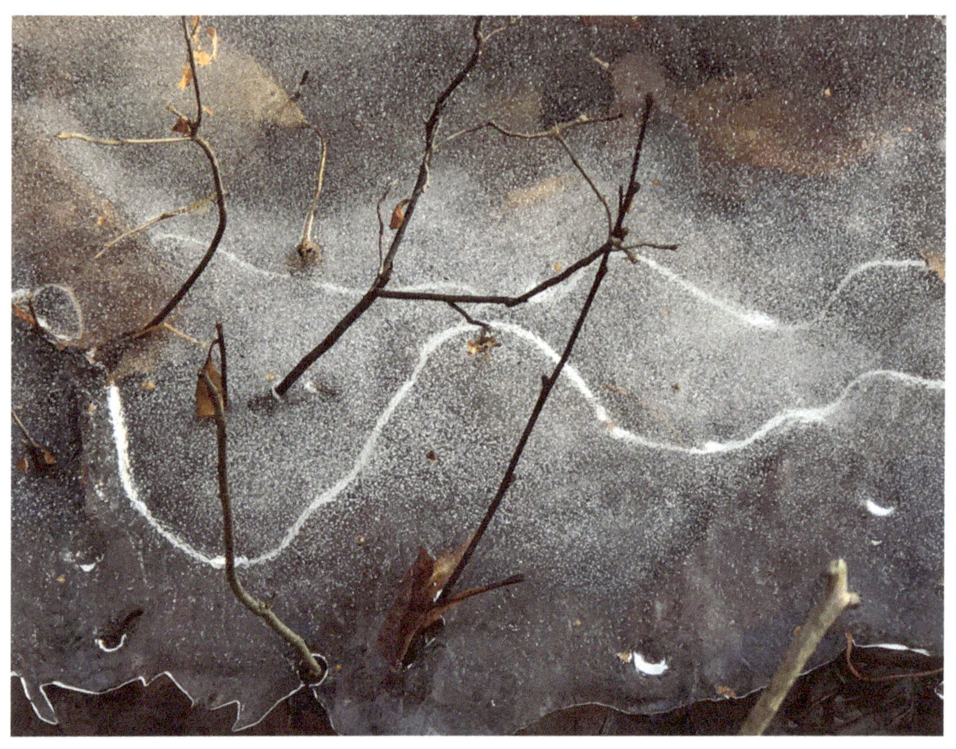

Trust that the moment will carry you
where you need to go.
Even a still pond is moving.

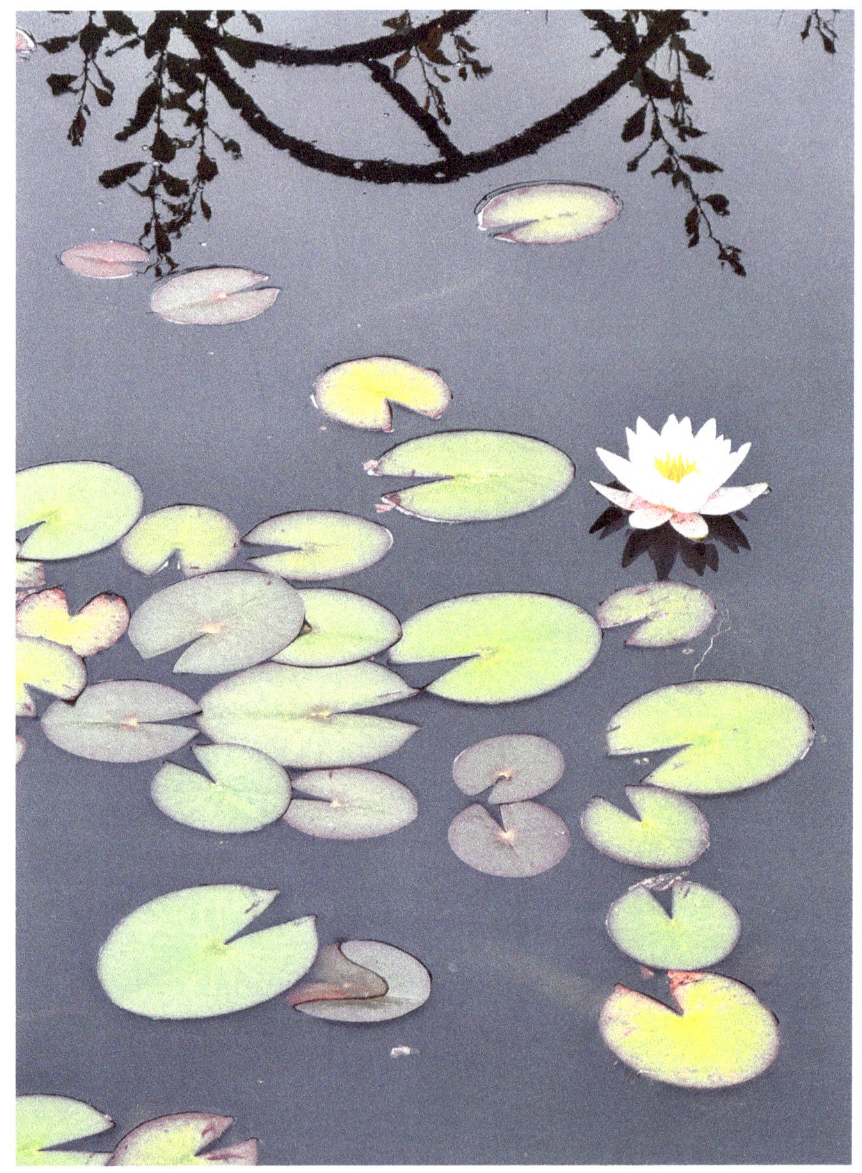

Care for every moment.

What you do matters.

What you say matters.

Every encounter matters.

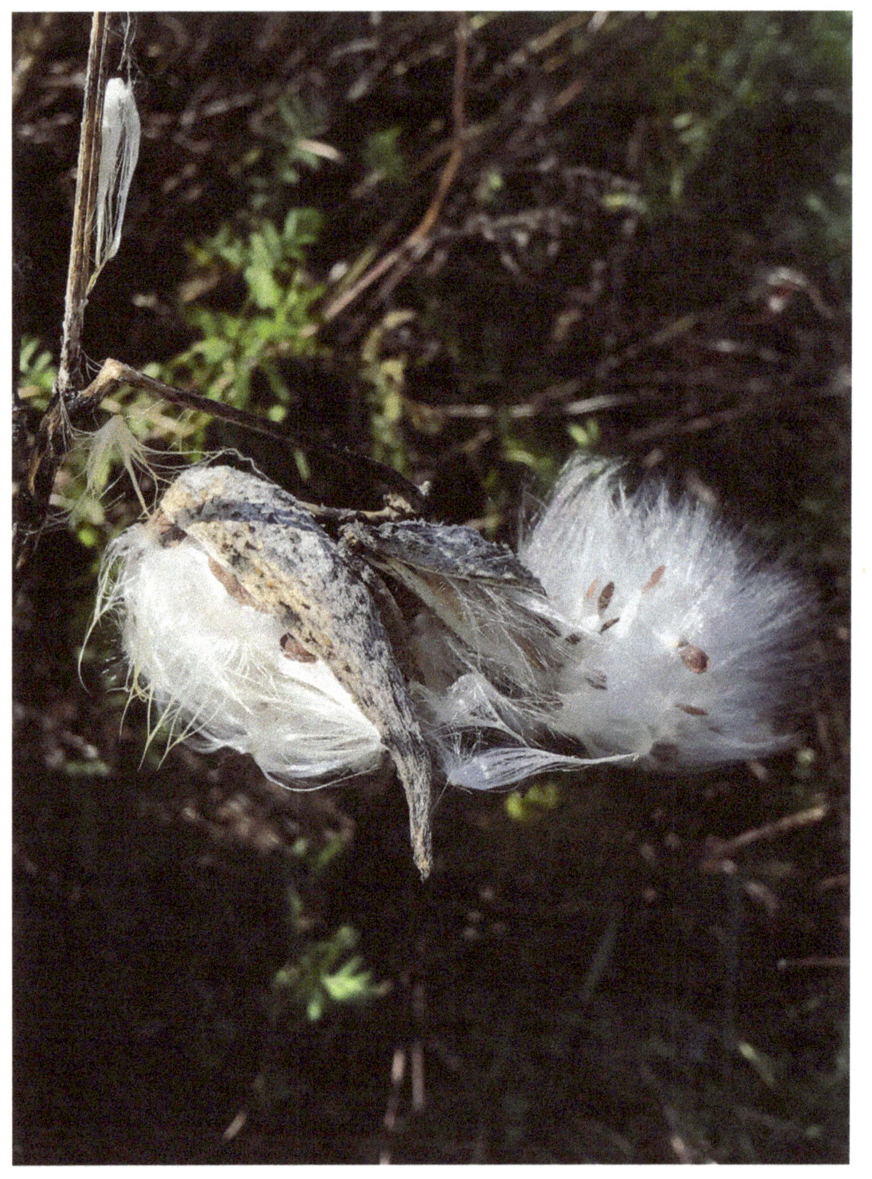

Trust.
Deep and steady trust.

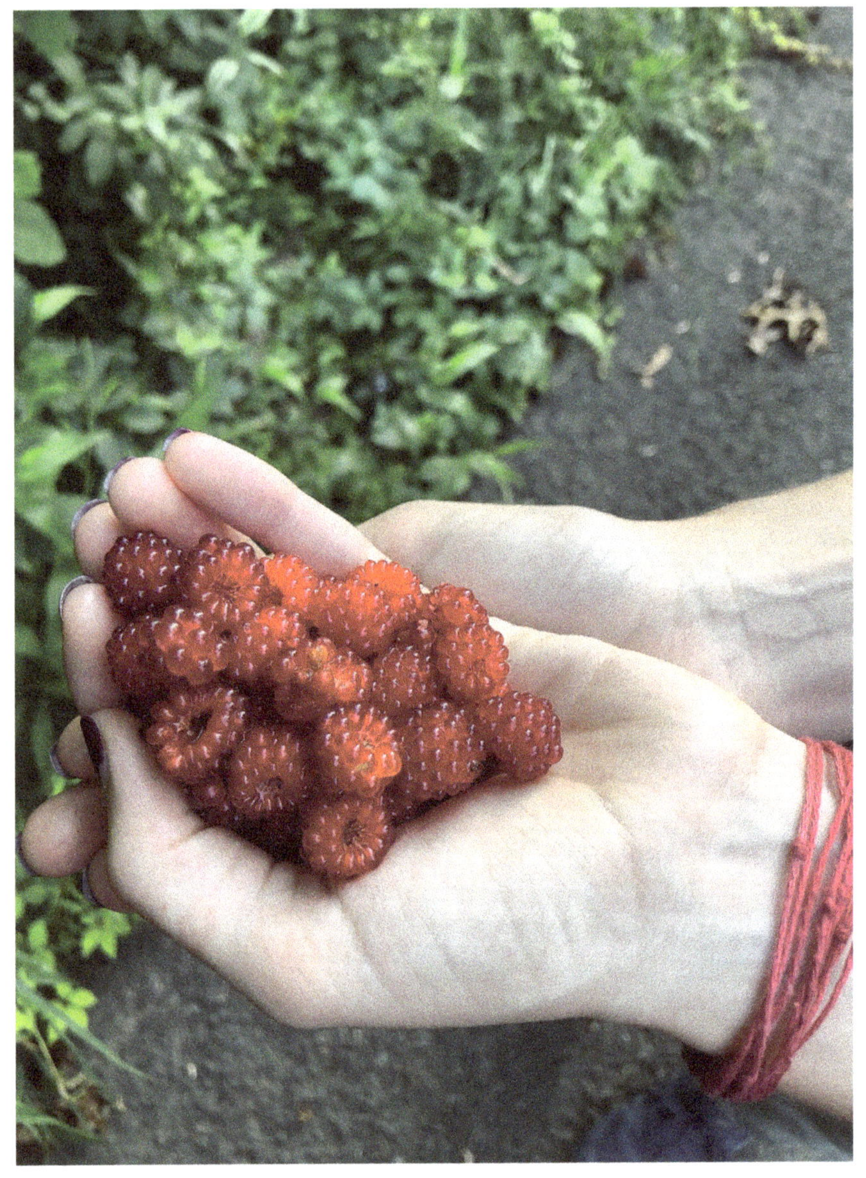

What does the next moment need from us?

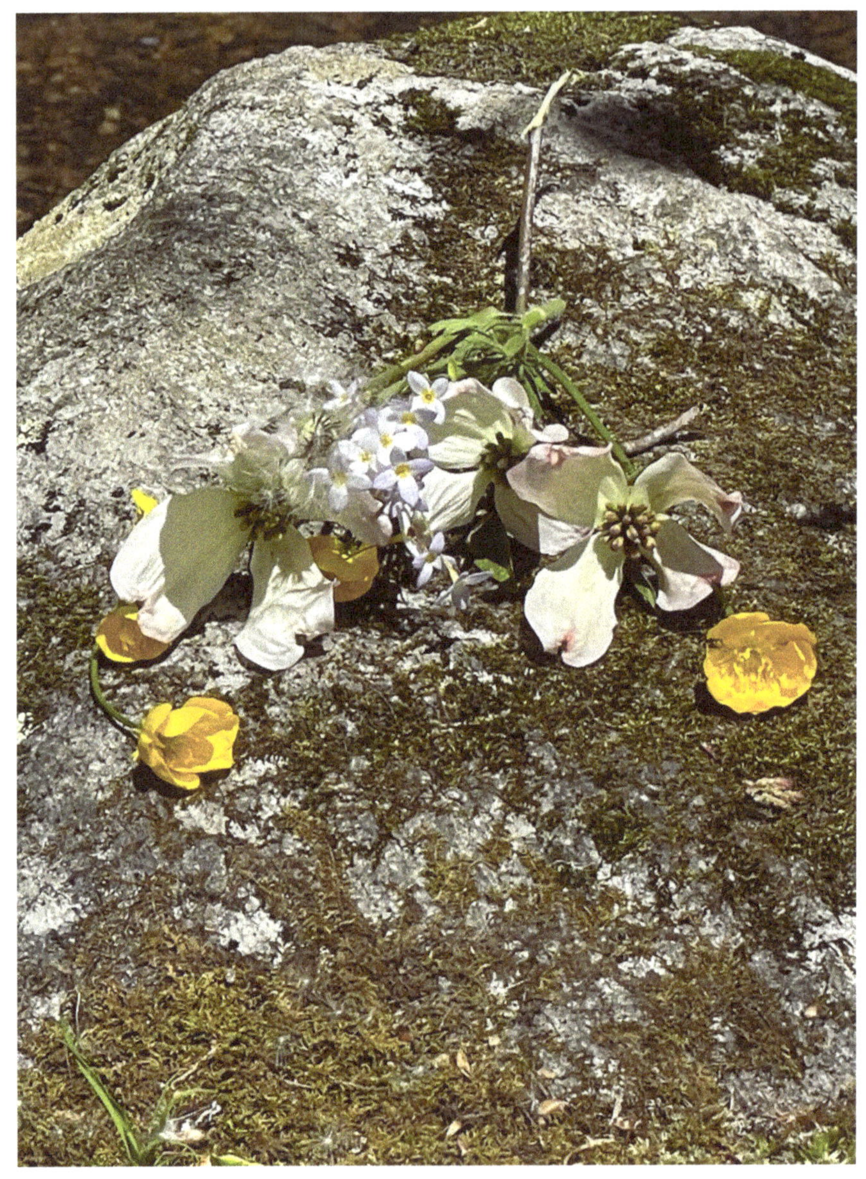

No words come close.
No words are needed.

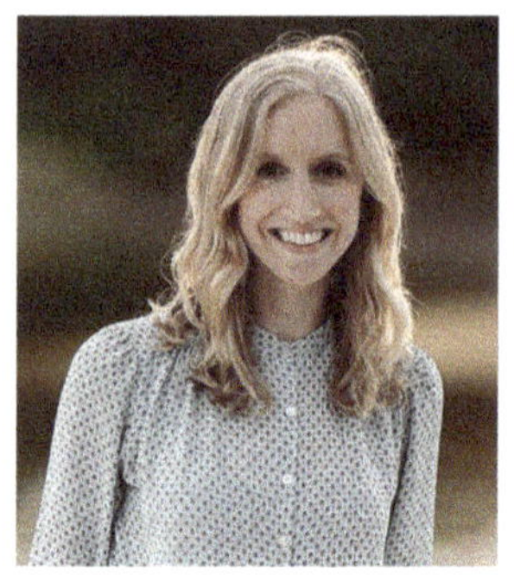

Marisa Mohrer, LCSW, MPH, is a Licensed Clinical Social Worker and EMDR Certified therapist in private practice. She holds a dual Master of Social Work and Public Health degree from the University of Pennsylvania. Mohrer specializes in therapy retreats for the healing of Complex PTSD. A longtime student of meditation teacher Tina Rasmussen, PhD, Mohrer now serves as a Professional Affiliate for Luminous Mind Sangha. She lives in Portland, Maine, and enjoys creative projects with her mom, Christina Giebisch. To learn more, visit marisamohrer.com.

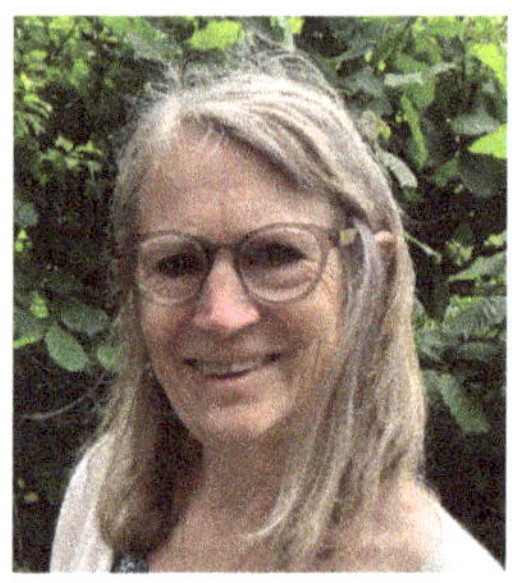

Christina Giebisch, LCSW, is a retired EMDR therapist and longtime meditator. A graduate of Yale University and Berkeley School of Social Work, she now enjoys pursuing her passion for photography and art making. Christina lives in Connecticut with her husband and three beloved pets.

With the deepest respect and humility, I attribute the inspiration of my texts to the teachings of the Buddha. I extend gratitude to my teacher Tina Rasmussen, who has been my guide on this path. Heartfelt recognition to Tara Brach and Rick Hanson, whose books and teachings inspired me to begin meditating. I offer a bow of appreciation to Stephen Mugen Snyder, Sharon Salzberg, Joseph Goldstein, and Jack Kornfield. I am immensely grateful for the expertise of Christine Cote at Shanti Arts Publishing for believing in this book and supporting its arrival into the world.

Daniella, I treasure our sisterhood. You have been here for me since day one. Lastly, this book would not exist were it not for the unconditional love of my mom and dad. At the heart of this book is their wisdom, generous spirit, and service to the world. No words can capture my gratitude and love for you both. Thank you for being who you are!

With Gratitude,
Marisa

❦

A special thank you to the two women whose influences are embedded in this collaborative venture with Marisa: Michaela Hauser-Wagner for her gentle dare to photograph daily, and Jan Blencowe for her encouragement and challenge to show up faithfully to artmaking.

Marisa, your spirit captures Light and reflects it back to all of us!

With Love,
Christina

SHANTI ARTS

NATURE ▪ ART ▪ SPIRIT

Please visit us online
to browse our entire book catalog,
including poetry collections and
non-fiction books on nature, healing,
art, and more.

Also take a look at our highly
regarded art and literary journal,
Still Point Arts Quarterly, a feast for
the eyes and the imagination —
available to download for free.

www.shantiarts.com